The MICROWAVE *Maestro*

By arrangement with GRANADA Television Ltd.

The MICROWAVE *Maestro*

How to use your microwave safely and imaginatively

KEVIN WOODFORD

Kevin Woodford, presenter of Granada TV's
Microwave Maestro is co-owner of the
prestigious WOODFORD'S restaurant
overlooking Douglas bay on the Isle of Man.
His partners are Robert and Sue Sangster.

He is the presenter and co-author of BBC's
The Reluctant Cook and broadcasts
regularly on regional TV and radio.

Front cover and inside photography: James Murphy
Stylist: Cathy Sinker
Home economist: Alyson Birch
Book design by Bill Mason

Published by BBC Books,
a division of BBC Enterprises Limited,
Woodlands, 80 Wood Lane, London W12 0TT
First Published 1990
© Kevin Woodford 1990
ISBN 0 563 20903 8

Set in Trump Mediaeval
by Ace Filmsetting Ltd, Frome, Somerset
Printed and bound in Great Britain by Richard Clay Ltd, Bungay, Suffolk
Colour separations by Dot Gradations Ltd, Chelmsford, Essex
Cover printed by Richard Clay Ltd, Norwich

CONTENTS

DEDICATION

For Jeannie, Steven and Janine for their
inspiration and support
and
for Eunice.

I would also like to thank Marian Nelson,
my producer, for her frank and honest
comments, Julian Flanders for his
constant, vigilant editorial guidance,
Frank Phillips, the book designer, and
Suzanne Webber for her advice and
wisdom.

Introduction

Not so long ago if anyone mentioned microwave cookery to me I would cringe and reject the concept totally.

I was of the opinion that this little high-tech culinary whizzbox was to be used solely for urgent defrosting, presumably because the cook had failed to remove it from the freezer the day before the item was to be cooked, and for reheating pre-cooked meals to order as and when members of the family arrived home.

Having been given the challenge to explore the machine's use more fully I can confidently state that it is quite capable of performing some of the most classical recipes, with slight adaptation, extremely well.

My view of the microwave is not as the sole piece of cookery equipment in a kitchen (although for many it could quite easily be) but more as an aid. And if used in conjunction with conventional equipment it gives great flexibility to the whole art of cookery.

What are microwaves and how do they cook food?

The microwave oven is capable of defrosting, cooking and re-heating foods at a phenomenal speed. So how does it work?

The oven itself is a metal-lined box which is capable of converting electric current into microwaves by means of a fuse known as a magnetron. Microwaves are high frequency electromagnetic waves of energy similar to radio, radar and television signals. They are often treated with unnecessary caution, since they are both non-ionising and non-accumulative and therefore not harmful.

There are basically three key stages to microwave cookery: reflection, transmission and absorption. Once food is placed in the oven, the door shut and the machine switched on, then microwaves are generated and directed into the metal oven cavity by means of a wave guide. The first stage occurs. As the walls are metal, the waves are unable to pass through and are REFLECTED. They therefore bounce off the walls in a regular pattern and are evenly distributed by a stirrer fan. The second stage, TRANSMISSION, is when the waves pass through the container holding the food. (This is why you cannot use a metal container; the waves would simply bounce off and not reach the food.) Finally, ABSORPTION occurs. The microwaves penetrate the food to a depth of about 2 in (5 cm) and an internal conduction process begins with each layer of food heating up the next.

The effect is that the microwaves heat the food without heating the oven cavity. The waves are absorbed by the moisture molecules within the food. The molecules are distributed and vibrate at a rate of over 2000 million times per second, generating intense heat within the food itself.

Not all food will cook at the same rate. Foods which are high in fat, sugar, moisture or air will cook much faster than foods which are denser in composition simply because it will take longer for the conduction process to penetrate the food.

Since it is the microwaves produced by the magnetron which vibrate the moisture molecules within the food, it follows that once the magnetron is switched off (either by the power being switched off or the oven door being opened) the waves immediately cease to be generated. But – and this is the clever bit that most people forget, or worse, ignore – the heat generated by means of conduction will still carry on cooking the food for a short time. This is why many recipes recommend a 'standing time', which will be explained in more detail later.

Microwave power and oven settings

Particularly in view of the very short cooking times of many microwave recipes, it is very important to get to know your own microwave oven. That way you will ensure excellent results. There are a number of reasons for this.

One of the major differences between microwave and conventional cookers is that they do not have a standard power level. Microwave power output is measured in watts, and the higher the wattage, the faster it is possible to cook food. So food cooked on full power at 700 watts cooks twice as quickly as food cooked at 350 watts. However, timing can also be affected by such things as the cubic capacity of the oven cavity, so the actual performance of ovens of a similar wattage may vary.

The majority of microwave ovens sold today are either 600, 650 or 700 watts. The popular older models tend to have a power output of 400 or 500 watts.

Power Settings

All the recipes in this book are based on a power output of not less than 600 watts. Therefore:

HIGH indicates full power output of 600 to 700 watts;

MEDIUM indicates 60 per cent of full power;

LOW indicates 35 per cent of full power.

Before you start cooking, check the correct settings for your own microwave and mark them in the book, so that you can be sure of successful results. The calculation is quite simple.

Settings for 600- to 700-Watt Ovens

Whatever the wattage of your microwave, use the maximum setting for HIGH.

To calculate the MEDIUM and LOW settings, multiply the percentage power required by the number of settings on your cooker and divide by 100.

MEDIUM power is 60 per cent, therefore:

$$\frac{60 \times \text{number of cooker settings}}{100} = \text{correct setting.}$$

LOW power is 35 per cent, therefore:

$$\frac{35 \times \text{number of cooker settings}}{100} = \text{correct setting.}$$

Settings for 400- to 500-Watt Ovens

If the power output of your oven is less than 600 watts, then you will need to allow longer cooking, thawing and standing times for all the recipes.

For a 400-watt oven add 15 to 20 seconds per minute.

For a 500-watt oven add 10 to 15 seconds per minute.

Personal Oven Details

Make a note of the correct settings for your own oven (and remember to alter them if you buy a new one). Then experiment with your cooking and you will soon begin to master the art of timing. Two important tips to help you get good results are to remember the standing time – food continues to cook when removed from the oven – and to check food before the end of cooking time – you can always return it to the oven for a few seconds more.

> **Make and model:** *PRO LINE M3030*
>
> **Power output:** ...... *700* ......
>
> **Number of cooker settings:** *9*
>
> **Medium power setting:** ......
>
> $$\frac{60 \times 90}{100} = \quad \text{5·4}$$
>
> **Low power setting:** ......
>
> $$\frac{35 \times 90}{100} = \quad \text{3·15}$$
>
> **Additional time allowance:** ......

Selecting a microwave oven

As with all appliances, there is a wide range of machines available and selection is dependent on personal requirements. To start with you will need to consider your budget, the space available and whether your microwave will be free-standing or built-in. Then you need to think about how you are going to use the oven, remembering that until you start to experiment it is difficult to realise the full range of the microwave's possibilities. If you are only cooking for one, a smaller capacity may suit. If you are going to use the oven regularly for a family, think bigger. There are plenty of other non-essential features you can choose, too, such as auto-sensor cooking or auto-defrost. Or you may want to go to the top of the range and choose a combination oven. Once you have made your selection, do be sure to check that the machine complies with all the safety requirements (it will usually state this very clearly) and that once the guarantee has expired, servicing, and in particular parts, are easily obtainable.

Microwave Features
Here are some of the features to look for.

- All standard models are equipped with the essential controls to induce power and start and stop the cooking process.

- All models have a timing control.

- All models have a power level control, but the number of settings will vary.

- The oven capacity varies between models.

- The majority of ovens now have a defrost control. This ensures that a low level of energy is generated so as to thaw frozen food without cooking it. It is also possible to slow cook using this power setting.

- Most machines now include a turntable. These are usually made of ceramic glass and are removable for ease of cleaning. They rotate during cooking to assist in cooking the food evenly and prevent parts of the food being held in a hot spot.

- Some models have a 'Delay/Stand' feature so that you can pre-set the microwave to delay cooking, or set standing times between programs.

- A browning control is a feature of some machines.

- A rotating antenna is fitted in some machines. This microwave distributor is designed to achieve more even cooking. It is usually housed above the oven ceiling or below the floor.

- Some models have an automatic re-heating programme.

- The latest feature which is ideal for the reluctant cook is the auto-sensor. It allows you the opportunity of determining your own culinary successes as you would with a normal microwave oven, or you can simply put the food inside the oven and press the relevant category of food on the auto-sensor button. The machine calculates the required cooking time by measuring the amount of steam released and the air temperature. As soon as the cooking time has been calculated, the remaining cooking time is displayed, and the cooker simply switches itself off when the cooking is complete.

- More expensive models also have an auto-defrost facility.

- The most expensive models may have an auto-sensor defrost/cook so that the oven will cook food straight from the freezer.

Combination Ovens

But perhaps you are looking for something a little more adventurous, capable of crossing the barrier between microwave and conventional cooking.

The combination oven could be just the thing. As its name implies it combines microwave facility with conventional electric oven all within the same oven cavity. The two can be used in unison, thus giving the speed and nutritional advantage of microwave cooking, and the colour and finish of conventional cooking, or they can be used separately.

Advantages of using a microwave oven

The most obvious advantage of using a microwave oven is the speed at which it can cook the food – the obvious example being a steamed syrup pudding which can be served after only 7 or 8 minutes. The size limitation can be restricting, however, since only one dish can be cooked at a time. But there are other benefits.

- It is multifunctional – it can steam, poach, boil, roast, bake and will, with the aid of a browning dish, even grill.

- The cooking times are so short that they mean a saving in terms of energy, which makes microwave cooking very economical.

- As they operate from a 13-amp socket and are so compact, they can be sited even in the smallest kitchen. This also makes them very versatile. You could even take your microwave on holiday with you.

- They come into their own when it comes to cleaning. Firstly many dishes can be cooked using the same container for preparation, cooking and serving. Secondly, the ovens themselves require only a light wipe over with a damp cloth. No hard burnt bits of food to fight with!

- For the busy household the microwave offers flexibility and a responsive approach to meal times. Food can be cooked, plated, covered and left for each member of the family to re-heat as and when required (not a very sociable approach to dining, but for some the only way).

- As microwave cooking requires very little liquid it preserves texture, flavour and also retains more valuable nutrients. In fact it is a very healthy method of cooking as very little added fat is required.

- From the safety aspect, there is little danger of the cook being burnt as there is no direct heat.

- Cooking odours and condensation are kept to a minimum, making the kitchen a more pleasant environment in which to work.

- Additional uses of the microwave include defrosting and re-heating prepared dishes directly from the freezer.

As the sole piece of cooking equipment in a kitchen, the microwave has limitations which are far superseded by its benefits. Used as an additional item of equipment alongside conventional equipment, it improves kitchen efficiency which in turn leads to better cooking.

Essential facts for good microwave cooking

It is an acknowledged fact that a microwave oven will cook many foods in 'next to no time', but what factors affect just how quickly an item of food will cook, and what factors will slow down the process? Here are a few pointers.

The Oven

We have already looked at the importance of knowing the wattage of your machine so that you can use the correct setting for the recipes of your choice. In the same way as you have developed an understanding of your conventional oven, you will eventually do the same with your microwave oven.

Hot Spots

Some ovens have 'hot spots' in which food will cook more quickly than others, although with stirrer fans and turntables this problem should be limited. You can take this into account when placing food in the oven. The simple method of 'hot spotting' is to place several small identical-sized dishes each filled with the same amount of water into the oven. Heat on full power and watch to see which boils first – *voilà*, a hot spot.

The Composition of Foods

Foods which have a high content of sugar or fat will cook or re-heat far more quickly than those with low amounts of these ingredients because fat and sugar absorb microwave energy very quickly. You will be unlikely to forget this when cooking jams or sweet puddings, but it also needs to be considered when cooking or re-heating dishes filled with hidden jam, sweetened fruit fillings and so on. Many tongues have learnt the hard way that warm pastry may contain boiling jam, so be warned!

Other foods are more delicate and therefore require TLC – 'tender loving cooking'. Items such as eggs, cheese, fish or cream can very easily be ruined by overheating.

Soups and other high-moisture foods will take longer to cook than foods which are cooked with just their own moisture. It is therefore wise to add only a minimal amount of liquid, for example, when cooking vegetables. They require just enough to add to their own moisture.

Temperature

Just as with any form of cooking, the colder the food is at the 'starting to cook stage' then the longer it will take to cook. This is why you should cook using the recipes as guidelines and rely not only on them and your watch, but also your experience as it develops.

You will note for example in this book when adding stock it says 'stock, hot'; this is to speed up the cooking process.

Size, Shape and Density

Where the opportunity exists (with vegetables, for example), it is important to cut, slice or chop the ingredients to similar sizes and shapes. Obviously there are many examples of foods which have predetermined shapes and so it is impossible to do this. The general rule in such cases is to place the food so that the thickest section is to the outer edge of the plate with the thinnest parts at the centre.

In cases where there is a part of the food which is vulnerable and needs extra care (asparagus is a good example), then it is worth considering shielding the section with thin pieces of foil, dull side out.

The single most important factor in establishing the length of time required to cook an item of food is its density. Foods which are tight and deep in texture will take longer to cook than those which are light, even if they are comparable in size or weight.

There was a theory that with microwaved food the item was cooked from the centre out. The fact is that the microwave energy will only affect 2 in (5 cm) below the surface, the remainder of the food is cooked as the heat is conducted through the layers towards the centre. With dense foods, the centre is therefore the last part to be cooked. Meat, for example, often needs to stand after cooking to allow the centre to cook.

Quantities of Food

When using a conventional oven the amount of time needed to cook a certain item is not affected by the number of items in the oven at that time. But in a microwave oven one bowl of soup will re-heat much faster than four. This is because there is a set amount of microwave energy generated and the more items the less energy available per item.

This is an important factor to consider if you are following a recipe but cutting down or increasing the portions. For example, if you halve a recipe then you should also reduce the cooking time by about one-third. It's best to test the food at regular stages in order to avoid overcooking. As this is precision cuisine, it is better to undercook. You can always put the food back in the oven for a few extra minutes.

The Dish

The shape and size of the dish used is an important factor in considering the length of time an item of food will take to cook. You will find full information on this in 'Tools and equipment'.

Micro techniques and tips

In view of the fact that the principles of microwave cookery are vastly different to those of conventional cookery, there are a number of guidelines worthy of note. These are simple techniques aimed at ensuring that the microwaved foods have a similar finish to conventionally cooked foods.

Arrangement and Rearrangement of Food

The siting of food inside the oven cavity is crucial for successful microwave cookery. The thicker, denser items should be arranged outermost with the thinner less dense foodstuffs to the centre, so that they will receive less microwave energy and consequently cook more slowly.

If you are cooking more than one of the same item, then arrange them on a plate or dish in a circle near the edge, with sufficient space between each item. This will enable the microwaves to cook all parts of each item of food evenly. When cooking food in a bowl or dish, make sure that the food is of an even depth. Because microwaves are less 'energetic' in the centre of the dish, where possible place an upturned cup in the middle to disperse the food to the outermost part of the dish or mould, or better still use a ring mould. Obviously this is not always possible so be sure to move the dish around during cooking and if necessary shield the edges to prevent them from overcooking.

What you cannot afford to do with a microwave oven is to place food in, switch on and expect miracles to happen. During cooking it is important to alter the position of food slightly or even turn it over. This will ensure that the food is cooked evenly and that no one part is subjected to overcooking from a hot spot (sounds more like a TV quiz game than a cooking process).

Covering

Covering food will not only prevent it from drying out, thus retaining moisture and speeding up the cooking process, but it will also stop the food from splashing and help to keep the oven cavity clean. In the majority of cases recipes for conventionally cooked foods which require covering with a lid would require covering in a microwave oven. The only difference would be in the type of covering that can be used. Casserole dishes with lids are ideal, providing they are non-metallic. Alternatively you can use a plate, saucer, bowl, microwave cling film or a plastic bag. The last two need a little hole making in them to allow the steam to escape and it is a good idea with microwave cling film to fold back one corner. This not only allows the steam to escape, but also facilitates stirring.

Foods which require a dry appearance when cooked, such as bread and cakes, can be cooked uncovered; whilst foods of a greasy composition are best covered with absorbent kitchen paper.

Commercially produced boiling and roasting bags are ideal not only for cooking meat, but also for vegetables.

The traditional method of cooking 'in a parcel' can be successfully carried out. Whole fish or meat can be wrapped in greaseproof paper with the edges well sealed by folding over. The flavours and juices are retained inside this 'parcel' during cooking.

Stirring

As with arranging and rearranging food, it is important with foods containing a high proportion of moisture to stir frequently during cooking. The centre should be drawn to the outside and vice versa, so that the heat is distributed to the centre.

Browning

One of the main criticisms of food cooked in a microwave oven is that it has not browned or coloured. This is a problem which to a certain degree can be overcome. We are conditioned through habit into the belief that certain cooked foods should have a specific appearance and why should we change the habit of several lifetimes for the sake of culinary technology?

Worry not. There are ways around this problem. Roasting bags will help brown poultry and joints of meat and a browning dish will do the same for smaller cuts such as chops and steaks. There are various special microwave seasonings available which, when sprinkled on the surface of meat and poultry, it is claimed, will give a golden appearance.

A simple method is to brown the food under a grill before or after cooking it in the microwave, or seal it in a frying pan on the stove.

For the sweeter aspects of cooking, careful selection of ingredients can lead to a more appetising appearance. Wholewheat rather than white flour can be used in cakes, pastry and bread. Top the finished goods with colourful garnishes such as chopped browned nuts or desiccated coconut. Bread can be finished with poppy seeds, cracked wheat or oatmeal prior to baking.

Shielding

Food which is of irregular shape will not cook to the same degree throughout unless shielded. This simply means covering the thinnest, least dense parts of the food with a very small piece of foil, dull side uppermost. It may seem confusing since the guidelines insist that no metal should be used in the oven cavity, but this is one exception to the rule. But do note that the amount covered should not exceed the amount uncovered and nor should it touch the internal sides of the oven cavity.

Foil can be placed over vulnerable parts of the food in order to protect it for the whole cooking period if necessary, but it is usually only needed for a part of the time. It can be added at the beginning or nearer the end, as required.

Where possible eliminate the need for shielding by reshaping food. Poultry, for example, can be trussed and fish double-layered at the thinnest part.

Piercing

As the moisture is heated during cooking, a considerable amount of steam can develop, so it is essential to pierce any covering to allow this to escape. This not only applies to microwave cling film and bags but also to skin- and membrane-covered food: potatoes, kidneys, liver and raw egg yolk to name just a few.

Standing Time

Food continues to cook by conduction once it has been removed from the microwave oven or the power has been switched off. It is this period which many recipes refer to as 'leave to stand for x minutes'.

Taking food from the microwave oven while it still looks slightly undercooked will allow it to finish by conduction and therefore not become overcooked.

Checking

As with all forms of cookery it is an essential element, and part of the fun, to check to see if the food is cooked before serving it. In many of the recipes in microwave cookery books a standing time will be recommended. So in this case be patient, cover the food and wait. If after testing it isn't cooked to your liking (we're all different, thank goodness) then return it to the oven and give it another minute or two until it is 'as you like it'.

Safety

Historically there has been a fear of using microwaves in cooking. Yet the facts are clear. The waves produced are non-ionising, non-accumulative, they do not damage food chemically nor do they cause irreversible damage to cellular and chemical structures in the human body.

Microwave ovens have built-in safety precautions. The doors are fitted with special locks, seals and cut-out switches that automatically switch off the power the moment the door is opened. The microwaves are not produced unless the door is completely closed. Incidentally all microwave ovens are rigidly tested by the manufacturers. Look for the label confirming that the machine meets the requirements of the appropriate British Standard for electrical safety and microwave leakage levels and follow closely the manufacturers guide for safety.

It could quite easily be argued that there are greater risks involved in cooking with flames, electric rings and dry heat.

In many of the recipes you will note an instruction to stir, shake or alter the position of the food, and this cannot be over-emphasised. The microwave oven does not generate an even level of power within the cavity and so certain areas are exposed to greater energy than others, and this is why the repositioning of the dish is so important.

This book does not include guidelines for the reheating of prepared chilled meals as in my opinion it is essential to follow carefully the manufacturers' instructions normally given on the packet.

Personally I am very fond of my body and wouldn't knowingly subject it to anything which might cause it harm or discomfort (such as food poisoning). The motto being, 'If in doubt – throw it out'.

Siting the cooker

With the exception of the bathroom, you could literally site the microwave oven anywhere in the house that you wanted. Its versatility is due to the fact that it requires a 13-amp socket and takes up as much space as a portable television. But you must consider certain factors in order to safeguard the oven.

The vents must be clear. If, for example, they are situated at the top of the oven, then nothing should be placed over them, so this would prohibit you from siting the oven under a cupboard or large shelf. Equally it would be inappropriate to site the oven in an area where the air is likely to be hot. The magnetron is cooled by air drawn in through the inlet valves. To draw in hot air is not a good idea.

Cleaning and maintenance

As with any new item of equipment you should, on purchasing a microwave oven, carefully check it to ensure that there is no damage or scratches. In particular look closely at the oven door, seal and hinges and also the oven cavity which should be free from dents or scratches. Be sure that you have all the components and adhere to the manufacturer's installation instructions.

Your oven should give you trouble-free cooking providing you take care of it. This means using the oven for culinary purposes only – don't attempt to dry clothes etc. in the machine! Always leave a cup of water (changed regularly) in the oven as a safeguard in case it gets turned on accidentally. Don't use metal dishes or plates with metal rims or decoration in the machine. If you are shielding thin food, use the least amount of foil possible, place the shiny side against the food and keep it away from the walls of the oven.

Check periodically that the door seals and latches are not damaged, and should you discover a problem with them don't use the oven until it has been checked by an engineer.

One of the great pluses with a microwave oven for me is when it comes to cleaning it. It can be done whilst drinking a glass of wine – it's that easy! Be sure to disconnect it from the mains supply. For everyday cleaning, simply wipe over the interior with a damp cloth and then with a dry cloth. This includes the door seal. There is usually no need to use cleansing agents unless the manufacturer specifically recommends one.

If the oven walls have become excessively dirty, for whatever reason, then place a cup of water in an equal quantity of lemon juice and heat on HIGH for 4 to 6 minutes, wipe down and dry the oven cavity and that should do the trick. Don't attempt to scrape off any particles or use abrasive cleaners as you might damage the oven.

Turntables and shelves can be removed and washed with warm soapy water, dried and replaced.

Tools and equipment

The cookery accessories one can use to cook food in a microwave oven differ enormously from those used in conventional forms of cookery. There are of course 'designer' pieces made specifically for the microwave – items such as plate rings, plastic ramekins, roasting racks, muffin trays, plastic spatulas and spoons, pudding basins – in fact, the list is endless. But in general terms you would find most of the essential items already in use, perhaps for different purposes, in your own kitchen.

In determining whether a piece of equipment is suitable for microwave use it is necessary to consider whether the material will allow the microwaves to pass through it. It should not, therefore, contain any material that will reflect or absorb microwaves; it needs to be resistant to the heat likely to be generated from the food being cooked and it needs to be the right size and shape.

Under no circumstances should metal containers be placed inside the oven. This would cause arcing (sparks will fly) and can damage the oven walls. This in turn will alter the pattern of the microwaves and ultimately result in a less than effective oven. This includes containers with metal handles, trim, or even gold-painted decoration.

If you are not sure whether a particular dish or bowl is suitable then simply apply this little test. Sit a cup of cold water in the dish to be tested. Heat on HIGH for 2 minutes (if the dish is plastic, heat for 15 seconds only). If the water is hot and the dish cool then all is well. If, however, the dish is hot and the water cool then you should not use the dish as it contains a certain amount of moisture to which the microwaves are attracted and this will prevent the full microwave energy penetrating the food.

Perhaps the most revolutionary aspect of cooking food in a microwave oven is the facility of being able to cook in disposable containers. Roasting bags, which are ideal for cooking meat as they help it to brown slightly, pressed polystyrene and microwave cling film can all be used. But without question the most interesting point is that it is possible to prepare foods in a dish, freeze it and defrost, re-heat and serve all in the same dish (great news for the reluctant dishwasher).

Suitable Materials

Paper Plain white paper cartons, plates, cups and napkins can all be used in the microwave oven. Avoid using coloured material as the dyes can run and discolour the food.

Absorbent kitchen paper is good for covering foods likely to 'splash' during cooking and for placing food on where there is a likelihood of excess moisture needing to be soaked up. Greaseproof paper is excellent for lining baking tins and can also be used to cover food. Wax-lined cardboard is not suitable for use in cooking due to the possibility of the heat melting the wax. This problem also exists with waxed cups.

Plastic For short cooking times the rigid plastic bowls, which are known to be dishwasher safe, are normally perfectly safe to use in the microwave oven. There is a wide range of plastic microwave cookware available. Empty margarine tubs and yoghurt pots and other such lightweight dishes will melt and are not satisfactory for cooking in, but they can be used to hold food while it is defrosting. Plastic cookware is not usually suitable for cooking foods with a very high fat or sugar content.

Glass Heatproof glassware is ideal for the microwave, because you are able to see the foods cooking and they allow easy transmission of the microwaves. Ordinary glassware is suitable for heating foods over short periods only, and it would be most unwise to attempt to use lead crystal in the microwave at all.

China, Pottery and Oven-to-Tableware Providing the dishes do not have metal trims, patterns or glued-on handles then they should be perfectly suitable for use in the microwave. It is best to avoid using antique china or fine porcelain as it may be damaged.

Unglazed earthenware is porous and is best avoided, but fully glazed earthenware and stoneware can be used, although food might take a little longer to cook in them.

Wood, Wicker and Straw Baskets made from these materials can be used in the microwave but be sure that they are not left in for long periods and that they have not been glued or wired in their construction. Extensive exposure of wooden spoons and bowls to microwave cooking can lead to them drying out and eventually cracking. This can be avoided by occasionally 'oiling' them with a little vegetable oil.

Linen Providing items are made from pure linen and contain no man-made (synthetic) fibres then they can be used for covering foodstuffs.

Browning Dishes These are specially-designed dishes that can be pre-heated, then used to brown foods.

Shapes and Sizes Round dishes are far more suitable for use in a microwave than oval, square or rectangular ones. This is because the food cooks more evenly due to even distribution of the microwaves. Shapes which have square corners will cause the microwaves to gather on these and this can lead to certain parts of the food being overcooked whilst other parts are uncooked.

When cooking with boiling water it is sensible to use deep bowls or dishes; this will prevent the water from spilling into the oven cavity.

Dishes with sloping or curved sides are not as effective as straight-sided dishes for even cooking. Wide, shallow dishes will allow food to cook more quickly than deep narrow ones.

Always use bowls which are sufficiently large to allow the liquid to rise up while cooking.

Defrosting at a glance

From 'freezer to microwave' – what a perfect combination for those wishing to limit vitamin loss in foods, whilst preserving the flavour and texture of the produce. It is economical and eliminates the need for much forward planning because the microwave can defrost food in a matter of minutes. Use the following charts as a general guide to successful defrosting.

MEATS

HELPFUL HINTS

- To speed the defrosting process, periodically drain away any liquid coming from the meat.

- If possible, use a microwave roasting rack when defrosting joints and remove any wrapping as soon as possible.

- Turn chops and steaks over during defrosting, as well as the larger joints of meat.

- A chop or steak is defrosted when it feels cold but is pliable to the touch.

- If a skewer can pass quite easily through the thickest part of the joint, it is defrosted.

Type	Time on low or defrost setting	Method
BACON AND PORK		
Bacon Rashers	2 minutes per 8 oz (225 g)	Remove from pack, separate when defrosted and stand for 6 to 8 mins.
Boned/Rolled Joint (Loin, Leg, Shoulder)	7 to 8 mins per 1 lb (450 g)	Turn periodically and allow meat to rest for 20 mins if it shows signs of cooking.
Chops	8 to 10 mins per 1 lb (450 g)	Separate whilst defrosting, putting thin ends to the centre.

Type	Time on low or defrost setting	Method
Joints on Bone	7 to 8 mins per 1 lb (450 g)	Turn periodically, leave to stand for 1 hour.
Sausages	5 to 6 mins per 1 lb (450 g)	Separate during defrosting. Stand for 5 mins.

BEEF

Type	Time on low or defrost setting	Method
Beefburgers 2 oz (50 g) 4 oz (100 g)	2 burgers – 2 mins 4 burgers – 2 to 3 mins 2 burgers – 2 to 3 mins 4 burgers – 4 to 5 mins	Can be cooked straight from freezer if preferred.
Boned Roasting Joint (Topside, Sirloin)	8 to 10 mins per 1 lb (450 g)	Turn over regularly whilst defrosting. Allow the meat to rest if it shows signs of cooking. Stand for 1 hour.
Joints on Bone (Ribs of beef)	10 to 12 mins per 1 lb (450 g)	Turn during defrosting. Stand for 1 hour to allow centre to thaw.
Minced Beef	8 to 10 mins per 1 lb (450 g)	Stand for 10 mins.
Steak (cubed)	6 to 8 mins per 1 lb (450 g)	Stand for 10 mins.
Steak (Sirloin, Rump)	8 to 10 mins per 1 lb (450 g)	Stand for 10 mins.

OFFAL

Type	Time on low or defrost setting	Method
Kidney	6 to 9 mins per 1 lb (450 g)	Separate whilst defrosting and stand for 5 mins.
Liver	8 to 10 mins per 1 lb (450 g)	Separate whilst defrosting and stand for 5 mins.

VEAL/LAMB

Type	Time on low or defrost setting	Method
Boned/Rolled Joints (Leg, Loin, Shoulder)	5 to 6 mins per 1 lb (450 g)	Turn regularly and rest the meat if it shows signs of cooking. Stand for 45 mins.
Chops	8 to 10 mins per 1 lb (450 g)	Separate whilst defrosting and stand for 10 mins.
Joints on Bone (Leg, Shoulder)	5 to 6 mins per 1 lb (450 g)	Turn regularly during defrosting. Stand for 1 hour to allow centre to thaw.
Minced Lamb/Veal	8 to 10 mins per 1 lb (450 g)	Stand for 10 mins.

FISH

HELPFUL HINTS

- To keep it moist, thaw fish in its freezer bag, but remember to pierce it first and finish defrosting in a bowl of cold water.

- Arrange prawns, scallops etc. in a circle and cover with absorbent kitchen paper to help soak up liquid. Remove immediately from the oven when defrosted.

Type	Time on low or defrost setting	Method
Non-oily White Fish Fillets (Cod, Haddock, Halibut)	4 to 7 mins per 1 lb (450 g)	Turn and rearrange thinnest parts to centre as soon as possible. Stand for 10 mins.
White Fish Steaks/ Cutlets	6 to 8 mins per 1 lb (450 g)	Turn during defrosting and separate as soon as possible. Stand for 10 mins.
Oily Fish (Mackerel, Kippers)	2 to 3 mins per 8 oz (225 g)	Stand for 5 mins after each 2 mins defrosting.
Prawns, Scampi, Shrimps	2 to 3 mins per 4 oz (100 g) 3 to 4 mins per 8 oz (225 g)	Separate as soon as possible. Stand for 2 mins and plunge into cold water.

POULTRY AND GAME

HELPFUL HINTS

- Thaw in freezer wrapping and pour off any liquid as it appears.

- Finish thawing in a bowl of cold water with the produce still in its bag.

Type	Time on low or defrost setting	Method
Chicken/Duck		
Portions	5 to 7 mins per 1 lb (450 g)	Separate whilst defrosting. Stand for 10 mins.
Whole	6 to 8 mins per 1 lb (450 g)	Remove giblets and any metal clips. Stand in bowl of cold water afterwards until thoroughly defrosted.

Type	Time on low or defrost setting	Method
Pheasant	5 to 7 mins per 1 lb (450 g)	As for chicken.
Turkey	10 to 12 mins per 1 lb (450 g)	Remove giblets and metal clips. Take bird out of oven and allow to rest for 10 mins several times. Stand in cold water afterwards until thoroughly defrosted.

BREAD AND BAKED PRODUCE

HELPFUL HINTS

- To avoid soggy bottoms, place baked goods on a double layer of kitchen paper which will absorb any excess moisture.

- In order to aid defrosting cakes, pies etc. they can be turned by a quarter every minute.

- For crisper bread, place it with absorbent paper on a microwave rack or upturned bowl to allow the air to circulate underneath.

Type	Time on low or defrost setting	Method
Bread		
Sliced – Large	6 to 8 mins	Turn whilst defrosting.
Small	4 to 6 mins	Stand 10 to 15 mins.
One slice	10 to 15 seconds	Time carefully, stand for 1 min.
Unsliced – Large	6 to 8 mins	As above.
Small	4 to 6 mins	
Bread Rolls, Tea Cakes, Crumpets, Scones, Croissants	15 to 20 seconds per 2	Time carefully. Stand for 2 to 3 mins.
Sponge Cake	1 to 2 mins per 1 lb (450 g)	Test and turn after 1 min. Stand for 5 mins.
Pastry (Shortcrust or Puff)	1 min per 8 oz (225 g)	Stand for 20 mins.

Basic cooking methods

HELPFUL HINTS

- The amount of food is important, make sure you know the weight, do *not* guess.

- Always underestimate the cooking time, and remember to cook with the heart as well as the watch. If it is underdone you can return it to the oven, whereas overcooking can ruin the produce.

- Produce which is high in fat or sugar will cook more quickly.

- The colder the produce is, the longer it will take to cook.

- If cooking irregularly shaped produce such as chops, chicken portions or fish, the thinner part should be placed towards the centre.

MEAT

Type	Time	Method
BACON AND PORK		
Bacon Joint	12 to 14 minutes per 1 lb (450 g) on HIGH	Cook covered. Turn during cooking. Wrap in foil and stand for 10 mins.
Bacon Rashers	1½ to 2 mins per rasher on HIGH	Cover with kitchen paper or greaseproof paper to prevent splashes. Remove paper immediately and stand for 2 mins.
Pork Chops	1 chop – 4 to 4½ mins on HIGH 2 to 4 chops – 5 to 8 mins on HIGH	Thinnest ends to centre. Turn during cooking. To colour cook in pre-heated browning dish or brown under grill after microwaving.
Sausages	2 to 4 sausages – 2 to 4 mins on HIGH	Pierce the skins before cooking and turn during cooking. Browning as for chops.
Pork Joint On the bone (roasting)	8 to 9 mins per 1 lb (450 g) on HIGH	Turn during cooking. Wrap in foil and stand for 15 mins.
Boned roasting joint	8 to 10 mins per 1 lb (450 g) on HIGH	Turn during cooking. Wrap in foil and stand for 15 mins.

Type	Time on low or defrost setting	Method
BEEF		
Joint		
On the bone (roasting)	5 to 8 mins per 1 lb (450 g) on HIGH	Turn during cooking. Wrap in foil and stand for 15 mins.
Boned roasting joint	5 to 9 mins per 1 lb (450 g) on HIGH	Turn during cooking. Wrap in foil and stand for 15 mins.
Mince	5 mins per 1 lb (450 g) on HIGH	Cover whilst cooking. Stand for 5 mins.
Steak (Rump, Fillet)	3 to 4 mins per 8 oz (225 g) on HIGH	Turn whilst cooking. Stand for 2 mins.
OFFAL		
Kidney	2 or 3 – 3 to 5 mins on HIGH	Prick before cooking. Stand for 5 mins.
Liver	5 to 6 mins per 1 lb (450 g) on HIGH	Cover whilst cooking. Stand for 5 mins.
VEAL/LAMB		
Chops	1½ mins on HIGH, plus 1½ mins on MEDIUM per 8 oz (225 g)	Place thin ends to centre. Brown as for pork chops. Stand for 2 mins.
Joints		
On the bone	6 to 9 mins per 1 lb (450 g) on HIGH	Place fatty side down and turn during cooking. Wrap in foil and stand for 15 mins.
Boned	6 to 9 mins per 1 lb (450 g) on HIGH	Turn during cooking. After cooking wrap in foil and stand for 15 mins.
Breast	6 mins per 1 lb (450 g) on HIGH. Use roasting rack to allow fat to drain.	Stand for 5 mins.

FISH

Type	Time	Method
Cutlets, Steaks, Fillets	4 mins per 1 lb (450 g) on HIGH	Turn and reposition during cooking as required.
Oily Fish (Kippers, Mackerel)	2 to 3 mins per 8 oz (225 g) on HIGH	Stand for 5 to 10 mins, covered.
Whole Flat Fish (Plaice, Sole)	3 mins on HIGH	Lightly score skins before cooking. Shield tail. Turn dish during cooking.
Whole Round Fish (Whiting, Small Haddock, Bream, Mullet)	4 mins per 1 lb (450 g) on HIGH	As for whole flat fish above.

RICE AND PASTA

HELPFUL HINTS

- Always cover rice or pasta with at least 1 in (2.5 cm) of boiling water.
- Cooking rice or pasta in a microwave will not save time but helps them remain separate, light and fluffy.

Type	Time	Method
Rice		
Brown	20 to 25 mins per 4 oz (100 g) on HIGH	Stir periodically during cooking. Stand for 10 mins and drain.
White long grain	10 to 12 mins on HIGH	As above.
Pasta		
Shapes	7 mins per 8 oz (225 g) on HIGH	Stir during cooking. Stand for 5 mins and drain.
Spaghetti, Tagliatelli Macaroni	8 mins per 8 oz (225 g) on HIGH	As above.

POULTRY AND GAME

Type	Time	Method
Chicken		
All chicken should be thoroughly cooked.		
Boned Chicken Breasts	2 to 3 mins on HIGH	Cook in covered dish. Turn during cooking. Can remove skins and brush in garlic/herb butter/margarine.
Chicken Portions	6 to 8 mins per 1 lb (450 g) on HIGH	Skin side up with thinnest part towards centre. Turn during cooking and stand for 5 mins.
Whole Chicken	8 to 10 mins per 1 lb (450 g) on HIGH	Cook in roasting bag, breast side down and turn during cooking. Stand for 15 mins.
Duck	8 to 10 mins per 1 lb (450 g) on HIGH	Prick duck skin all over before cooking. Place breast side down on roasting rack with dish underneath. Turn duck and empty dish periodically. Stand for 15 mins.
Pheasant	8 to 10 mins per 1 lb (450 g) on HIGH	Cook in roasting bag breast side down and turn during cooking. Be careful not to make it dry by overcooking. Stand for 5 to 10 mins.
Turkey	9 to 11 mins per 1 lb (450 g) on HIGH	Turn periodically, but begin with breast side down. Cover and stand for 20 mins.

FRESH VEGETABLES

HELPFUL HINTS

- Use a small amount of water (approximately 2 tablespoons) to retain nutrients, flavour and colour.
- The produce should be cut, when required, in *even*-sized pieces.
- Pierce vegetables with skins before cooking to prevent bursting.
- Season after cooking as salt used in the microwave has a drying effect.

Type	Time	Method
Artichoke (Globe)	2 medium – 7 to 8 mins on HIGH	Place upright in covered dish and add 6 tablespoons water.
Asparagus	7 to 8 mins per 1 lb (450 g) on HIGH	Place stalks to outside.
Aubergine (diced/sliced)	5 to 7 mins per 1 lb (450 g) on HIGH	Stir during cooking.
Beans Broad	6 to 8 mins per 1 lb (450 g) on HIGH	Stir during cooking.
Green (sliced)	10 to 13 mins per 1 lb (450 g) on HIGH	Stir during cooking.
Beetroot	7 to 12 mins per 1 lb (450 g) on HIGH	Pierce skins.
Broccoli	4 to 5 mins per 8 oz (225 g) on HIGH	Turn during cooking.
Brussels sprouts	4 to 5 mins per 8 oz (225 g) on HIGH	Stir during cooking.
Cabbage (shredded)	8 to 10 mins per 1 lb (450 g) on HIGH	Stir during cooking.
Carrots	8 to 12 mins per 1 lb (450 g) on HIGH	Stir during cooking.
Cauliflower (florets)	7 to 8 mins per 1 lb (450 g) on HIGH	Stir during cooking.
Cauliflower (whole)	9 to 12 mins on HIGH	Shake during cooking.
Celery	10 to 12 mins per 1 lb (450 g) on HIGH	Cut into small, equal slices.
Corn-on-the-cob (two)	7 to 8 mins on HIGH	Wash and trim.

Type	Time	Method
Courgettes	5 to 7 mins per 1 lb (450 g) on HIGH	Cut into small equal slices and cook in 1 tablespoon water.
Fennel	8 to 9 mins per 1 lb (450 g) on HIGH	Cut in equal slices.
Leeks	7 to 9 mins per 1 lb (450 g) on HIGH	Trim and slice into equal pieces.
Mangetout	7 to 8 mins per 1 lb (450 g) on HIGH	Shake during cooking.
Mushrooms	3 to 4 mins per 8 oz (225 g) on HIGH	In place of water add 1 oz (25 g) margarine or butter, a squeeze of lemon and, after cooking, a little black pepper.
Onions	3 to 4 mins per 8 oz (225 g) on HIGH	Slice into equal pieces.
Parsnips	6 to 8 mins per 1 lb (450 g) on HIGH	Peel and slice.
Peas	9 to 11 mins per 1 lb (450 g) on HIGH	Stir during cooking.
Potatoes Boiled	6 to 7 mins per 1 lb (450 g) on HIGH	Peel and cut into equal pieces.
Jacket – 4 × 6 oz (175 g)	12 to 15 mins on HIGH	Scrub and prick well before cooking. Turn during cooking.
Spinach	6 to 8 mins per 1 lb (450 g) on HIGH	Wash and shred. No water required.
Swede	6 to 8 mins per 8 oz (225 g) on HIGH	Peel and dice.
Tomatoes	2 to 3 mins per 8 oz (225 g) on HIGH	No water required. Quarter or slice.

About the recipes

Here are a few points to note about the recipes.

- Most recipes are designed to serve 4 people, unless otherwise specified.

- Follow one set of measurements only, do not mix metric and imperial.

- Spoon measurements are level.

- Size 3 eggs are used for the recipes.

- Cook uncovered unless directed otherwise.

- The bowl sizes used in the book are as follows:
Small bowl = about 1½ pints (900 ml);
Medium bowl = about 4 pints (2.25 l);
Large bowl = about 6 pints (3.4 l).

Soups and Starters

One of the most crucial factors when planning a menu for a dinner party is to include a starter which balances with the rest of the food to be served. Not only that but it must create the right impression so that everyone has confidence in the cook and consequently the dishes to follow, and allow the host or hostess to mingle with the guests for a pre-dinner drink. With only a conventional oven, this invariably restricts the starter to being either soup, which can tick away merrily on the stove until required, or alternatively a cold starter. But fear not. The wonder of the microwave oven dispenses with the restrictions imposed in the menu planning of the Dark Ages.

Because of their ability to re-heat quickly, adventurous hot starters can be prepared in advance and finished in seconds as your guests make their way to the table. Of course, careful menu planning is still vital. There must always be a balance between texture, colour, flavour and ingredients. But the microwave certainly extends the range of dishes that can be presented.

Glazed French Onion Soup

SERVES 4

2 oz (50 g) butter
1½ lb (750 g) onions, peeled and thinly sliced
2 cloves garlic, peeled and crushed
1 teaspoon chopped parsley
1 teaspoon crushed black peppercorns
1 bouquet garni
1 glass red wine
2 pints (1.2 l) beef stock, hot
4 slices French bread
3 oz (75 g) Gruyère cheese, grated
Salt and freshly ground black pepper

1. Place the butter in a large bowl and heat on HIGH for 1 minute. Add the onions, garlic, parsley and peppercorns.

2. Cover and cook on HIGH for 6 to 8 minutes.

3. Add the bouquet garni, red wine and hot stock, cover and cook on HIGH for 18 to 20 minutes. Stir at least twice during cooking.

4. Toast the French bread and then heap the grated cheese on top of each piece and brown it under the grill.

5. Season the soup, remove the bouquet garni and serve with the cheese on toast floating on the top.

CREAM OF WATERCRESS AND MUSSEL SOUP

SERVES 4

4 pints (2.25 l) mussels,
  scrubbed and debearded
¼ pint (150 ml) dry white
  wine
2 oz (50 g) butter
1 clove garlic, peeled and
  crushed
2 oz (50 g) onion, peeled and
  finely chopped
1½ oz (40 g) flour
1 pint (600 ml) milk
2 bunches of watercress,
  stalks removed and leaves
  well washed
Juice of ½ lemon
Salt and freshly ground
  black pepper
2 tablespoons cream

1. Place the mussels and wine in a large bowl, cover and cook on HIGH for 4 to 6 minutes. Make sure they are cooked by checking that the shells have opened. Discard any which remain closed.

2. Transfer the mussels into a conical strainer, drain and retain the cooking liquid for later use. Remove the mussels from the shells and put to one side.

3. Put the butter, garlic and onion into a large bowl and cook on HIGH for 2 minutes. Add the flour, mix well and cook on HIGH for a further 2 minutes, stirring occasionally.

4. Gradually add the milk and the cooking liquid from the mussels, lightly whisking to ensure a smooth texture. Add the watercress leaves, keeping back a small quantity for garnish, and cook on HIGH for a further 6 minutes.

5. Keep a few mussels for garnish, and add the remaining cooked mussels with the lemon juice. Pass the soup through a food processor, blender or conical strainer.

6. Season to taste and cook on HIGH for 1 minute to bring it to serving temperature.

7. Serve in bowls or a tureen, garnished with mussels and watercress, and 'dribble' the cream over the surface.

MULLIGATAWNY SOUP

SERVES 4

1 oz (25 g) butter

1 small onion, peeled and
finely diced

2 oz (50 g) carrots, peeled
and finely diced

1 clove garlic, peeled and
crushed

3 oz (75 g) celery, washed
and diced

2 oz (50 g) leeks, washed and
diced

2 oz (50 g) apple, cored and
diced (do not peel)

1 tablespoon curry powder
(or more to taste)

1 tablespoon tomato purée

1 oz (25 g) flour

1½ pints (900 ml) beef stock,
hot

½ oz (15 g) desiccated
coconut

Salt and freshly ground
black pepper

1 bouquet garni

1 oz (25 g) basmati rice,
cooked

Chopped parsley to garnish

1. Place the butter in a large bowl and heat
on HIGH for 45 seconds. Add the onion,
carrots, garlic, celery, leek and apple. Cover
and cook on HIGH for 4 to 5 minutes,
stirring at least once.

2. Add the curry powder, tomato purée and
flour, mix well, cover and cook on HIGH for
1 minute.

3. Gradually add the hot beef stock, mixing
thoroughly, and finally add the desiccated
coconut and bouquet garni.

4. Cook uncovered on HIGH for 12 to 14
minutes, stirring occasionally.

5. Remove the bouquet garni and pass the
soup through a food processor, blender or
conical strainer. Season to taste. Return to a
clean bowl, check and adjust the seasoning,
add the rice and cook on HIGH for 1 minute.

6. Serve garnished with parsley.

CLAM CHOWDER

SERVES 4

4 oz (100 g) potatoes, peeled and diced
1 oz (25 g) butter
4 oz (100 g) back bacon, rind removed and diced
4 oz (100 g) onion, peeled and chopped
1 × 8-oz (225-g) tin clams in brine, drained
½ teaspoon crushed black peppercorns
1 bay leaf
1 sprig of rosemary
¾ pint (450 ml) milk
Juice of ½ lemon
1 tablespoon chopped parsley
¼ pint (150 ml) double cream
Salt

1. Place the potatoes in a large bowl, barely cover with water, cover and cook on HIGH for 5 minutes until soft. Drain and keep to one side.

2. Put the butter into a large bowl and heat on HIGH for 45 seconds. Add the bacon and onion, cover and cook on HIGH for 5 to 6 minutes.

3. Add the potatoes, clams, black pepper, bay leaf and rosemary and cook on HIGH for 1 minute. Pour on the milk, lemon juice, parsley and cream, season lightly and cook on MEDIUM for 4 to 6 minutes until the soup is hot but not boiling.

4. Remove the bay leaf and rosemary. Check and adjust the seasoning if necessary, and serve immediately.

CELERY AND WALNUT SOUP WITH CREAMED STILTON

SERVES 4

1 oz (25 g) butter
3 oz (75 g) onion, peeled and
   finely diced
1 large head of celery,
   washed, trimmed and
   sliced
3 oz (75 g) walnuts, chopped
3 oz (75 g) potatoes, peeled
   and diced
2 pints (1.2 l) chicken stock,
   hot
1 bouquet garni
Salt and freshly ground
   black pepper
3 oz (75 g) Stilton cheese
3 fl oz (85 ml) double cream
1 teaspoon chopped parsley
4 walnut halves

1. Put the butter in a large bowl and heat on HIGH for 1 minute. Add the onion, celery, walnuts and potato, cover and cook on HIGH for 8 to 10 minutes.

2. Add the chicken stock and bouquet garni and season lightly. Cover and cook on HIGH for 20 to 22 minutes. Stir occasionally.

3. Allow the soup to cool slightly, remove and discard the bouquet garni and pass the soup through a food processor, blender or conical strainer. Place in a clean serving dish, check and adjust the seasoning if necessary.

4. Put the Stilton into a small bowl and heat on HIGH for 1 to 2 minutes until soft. Add the cream and mix together well.

5. Pour the creamed Stilton into the soup. Mix in well and place the soup in the oven on HIGH for 2 minutes.

6. Serve garnished with 4 walnut halves floating on the surface of the soup.

FARMHOUSE CHICKEN AND PRUNE SOUP

SERVES 4

2 oz (50 g) butter
8 oz (225 g) carrots, peeled
  and diced
4 oz (100 g) leeks, trimmed,
  washed and diced
4 oz (100 g) swede, peeled
  and diced
3 oz (75 g) celery, washed
  and diced
1 oz (25 g) plain flour
1½ pints (900 ml) chicken
  stock, hot
1 bouquet garni
Salt and freshly ground
  black pepper
8 soaked prunes, finely
  chopped
1 teaspoon chopped parsley

1. Place the butter in a medium bowl and heat on HIGH for 45 seconds.

2. Add the vegetables and lightly mix together. Cover and cook on HIGH for 8 minutes. Stir at least twice during cooking.

3. Add the flour and mix well. Stir in the hot stock, add the bouquet garni and season lightly with salt and pepper. Cook uncovered on HIGH for 15 to 18 minutes.

4. Add the prunes and cook on HIGH for a further 1 minute. Check and adjust the seasoning if necessary. Remove the bouquet garni, garnish with the chopped parsley and serve.

VICHYSSOISE

SERVES 4

1 oz (25 g) butter
2 medium leeks, washed,
  trimmed and finely sliced
1 onion, peeled and finely
  chopped
12 oz (350 g) potatoes, peeled
  and finely sliced
1¼ pints (750 ml) chicken
  stock, hot
1 bouquet garni
Salt and white pepper
¼ pint (150 ml) double
  cream
1 oz (25 g) chives, snipped

1. Put the butter in a medium bowl and heat on HIGH for 1 minute. Add the leeks and onion, cover and cook on HIGH for 6 to 8 minutes.

2. Add the potatoes, chicken stock and bouquet garni. Season lightly with salt and pepper. Cover and cook on HIGH for 16 to 18 minutes until the potatoes are soft. Stir at least twice during cooking.

3. Remove the soup from the oven and allow to cool. Discard the bouquet garni and pass the soup through a food processor, blender or conical strainer. Transfer to a clean serving dish and place in the refrigerator to chill.

4. Before serving add the cream, check and adjust the seasoning if necessary and garnish with the snipped chives.

CHILLED LEMON MINT AND CUCUMBER SOUP

SERVES 4

1 oz (25 g) butter
3 oz (75 g) onion, peeled and
  finely diced
1 clove garlic, peeled and
  crushed
1 bunch of watercress, leaves
  only, washed
1 teaspoon crushed black
  peppercorns
3 tablespoons chopped
  lemon mint
1 large cucumber, peeled and
  finely diced
1¼ pints (750 ml) chicken
  stock, hot
¼ pint (150 ml) single cream

1. Place the butter in a large bowl and heat on HIGH for 45 seconds. Add the onion and garlic and cook on HIGH for 6 to 8 minutes.

2. Add the watercress and peppercorns. Reserve a little lemon mint and diced cucumber for garnish and add the remainder. Add the stock, mix well and cook on HIGH for 5 to 7 minutes.

3. Allow the soup to cool and then pass through a food processor, blender or conical strainer. Place in a clean serving dish and refrigerate.

4. Once chilled, add the cream and mix in well. Check and adjust the seasoning if necessary.

5. Serve garnished with a little lemon mint and diced cucumber.

SALMON AND PRAWN MOUSSE WITH LEMON AND LIME SALAD

SERVES 4

6 oz (175 g) salmon, skin and
   bone removed
Juice of ½ lemon
2 fl oz (50 ml) dry white
   wine
½ oz (15 g) gelatine
A pinch of paprika
2 oz (50 g) prawns, cooked
   and peeled
6 fl oz (175 ml) double
   cream, lightly whipped
1 egg white, beaten to a peak
Salt and freshly ground
   black pepper
Juice of ½ lemon
4 leaves frisée, washed and
   torn
8 leaves lamb's lettuce or
   oak leaf lettuce, washed
   and torn
8 leaves radicchio
2 limes, segmented
1 lemon, segmented
½ pint (300 ml) plain
   yoghurt
Juice of ½ lemon
1 tablespoon chopped fennel
4 whole prawns, cooked
4 sprigs of fennel

1. Place the salmon in a large bowl with the juice of ½ lemon and the dry white wine and cook on HIGH for 3 to 4 minutes. Pour the cooking liquid into a clean bowl and leave the salmon to cool.

2. Add the gelatine to the wine and mix until dissolved.

3. Once the salmon is cool, break it into small enough pieces to go into the food processor or blender and whilst blending add the gelatine mixture, a pinch of paprika and the shelled prawns. Once the mixture is smooth, leave to cool.

4. Fold the lightly whipped cream into the mixture, then cut in the egg white using a metal spoon.

5. Season with salt and freshly ground black pepper and transfer the mixture into individual ramekins which have been very lightly greased. Place in the refrigerator to set.

6. Lay the prepared 'designer leaves' on 4 large plates and decorate with the lime and lemon segments. Leave a small space for the dressing.

7. Mix together the yoghurt, lemon juice and chopped fennel and season with salt and freshly ground black pepper.

8. Dip the ramekins into a bowl of warm water for a moment or two, taking care that the water does not go into the dish, and then turn out on to the lettuce. Garnish each mousse with a whole prawn and sprig of fennel and pour a little dressing on to the plate.

CHICKEN LIVER PÂTÉ

SERVES 4

1 tablespoon vegetable oil
2 oz (50 g) streaky bacon,
   rind removed and chopped
10 oz (275 g) chicken livers
2 cloves garlic, peeled and
   crushed
3 oz (75 g) onion, peeled and
   chopped
5 oz (150 g) butter
A pinch of tarragon
A pinch of rosemary
A pinch of sage
Freshly ground black pepper
1 small glass brandy
1 fl oz (25 ml) double cream

1. Place the oil in a large bowl and heat on HIGH for 1 minute. Add the chopped bacon and cook on MEDIUM for 2 minutes.

2. Add the livers, garlic, onion, 3 oz (75 g) of the butter, the herbs and black pepper to taste. Mix well. Cover and cook on MEDIUM for 6 to 7 minutes, stirring occasionally.

3. Add the brandy and cream and mix in well. Check and adjust the seasoning if necessary. Place in 4 small soufflé or ramekin dishes.

4. Melt the remaining butter in a small bowl on HIGH for 45 seconds, pour a little over each ramekin and allow to cool.

5. Refrigerate for about 4 hours before serving.

ROLLMOP HERRINGS WITH PEPPERED CREAM DRESSING

SERVES 4

1 large onion, peeled and
   sliced into thin rings
4 herrings, filleted
12 fl oz (350 ml) tarragon
   vinegar
1 teaspoon caster sugar
1 teaspoon freshly ground
   black pepper
1 teaspoon pickling spice
2 bay leaves
4 fl oz (120 ml) plain yoghurt
Juice of ½ lemon
1 teaspoon freshly ground
   black pepper
A pinch of cayenne pepper

1. Place the onion rings in a shallow dish.

2. Roll up the herrings, flesh inwards, and secure with a wooden cocktail stick. Place on top of the sliced onion.

3. Mix together the vinegar, sugar, black pepper, pickling spice and bay leaves and pour the mixture over the herrings.

4. Cover and cook on HIGH for 8 minutes, turning the plate after 4 minutes. Remove from the oven, leave to cool then refrigerate until required.

5. Mix together the yoghurt, lemon juice, pepper and cayenne to a smooth sauce to serve with the rollmops.

DEVILLED LAMBS' KIDNEYS

SERVES 4

2 oz (50 g) butter
8 oz (225 g) lambs' kidneys,
   skinned, cored and halved
3 oz (75 g) onion, peeled and
   finely diced
1 clove garlic, peeled and
   crushed
2 oz (50 g) mushrooms,
   sliced
1 teaspoon tarragon
1 teaspoon crushed black
   peppercorns
½ tablespoon tomato purée
½ oz (15 g) plain flour
1 small glass red wine
¼ pint (150 ml) beef stock,
   hot
1 teaspoon made English
   mustard (to taste)
1 drop tabasco sauce
1 teaspoon Worcestershire
   sauce
Salt and cayenne pepper

1. Melt 1 oz (25 g) of butter in a pan on the stove, add the kidneys and allow to colour lightly, then drain off the fat.

2. Place the remaining butter in a large bowl and heat in the microwave on HIGH for 45 seconds. Add the onion, garlic, mushrooms, tarragon and crushed black peppercorns. Cook on HIGH for 5 minutes, stirring twice.

3. Stir in the tomato purée and flour and mix well. Add the red wine, hot beef stock, mustard, tabasco sauce and Worcestershire sauce and mix well.

4. Place the kidneys into the sauce. Season lightly with salt and cayenne pepper. Cook on HIGH for 4 to 5 minutes.

5. Check and adjust the seasoning if necessary. Cover and leave to stand for 1 minute before serving.

CITRUS FRUIT IN BITTER ORANGE SAUCE

SERVES 4

2 oranges
2 limes
1 grapefruit
6 oz (175 g) granulated sugar
2 fl oz (50 ml) orange juice
¼ pint (150 ml) water
1 small glass cointreau
4 sprigs of mint

1. Remove the zest from the fruit without taking off the white pith, and cut the zest into very thin pieces (the easiest way is by using a zester).

2. Remove the white pith from the fruit and then carefully segment it by inserting a sharp knife between the membranes.

3. Arrange the fruit neatly in individual serving dishes and put to one side.

4. Place the zest from the fruit, the sugar, orange juice and water in a medium bowl and cook on HIGH for 8 minutes. Stir half-way through and keep an eye on the syrup whilst it is cooking.

5. Add the cointreau, mix it in well and pour it over the fruit. Garnish with the mint leaves and serve hot.

MUSHROOM CASSEROLE IN MEAUX MUSTARD SAUCE

SERVES 4

2 oz (50 g) butter
1 clove garlic, peeled and
   crushed
1 bay leaf
3 oz (75 g) onion, peeled and
   finely chopped
1 lb (450 g) mushrooms
Salt and freshly ground
   black pepper
1 teaspoon Meaux mustard
½ glass sherry
Juice of ½ lemon
¼ pint (150 ml) single cream
   or plain yoghurt
1 teaspoon chopped parsley
A pinch of paprika

1. Place the butter in a large bowl and heat on HIGH for 45 seconds. Add the garlic, bay leaf and onions and cook on HIGH for 2 minutes.

2. Add the mushrooms, season with salt and black pepper and cook on HIGH for a further 4 minutes. Add the mustard, sherry, lemon juice and cream or yoghurt and cook on HIGH for a further 4 to 6 minutes.

3. Remove the bay leaf. Check and adjust the seasoning to taste. Garnish with the chopped parsley and a light sprinkling of paprika over the surface of the sauce.

FISH AND SHELLFISH

I am convinced that the microwave was invented primarily to cook fish. The cooking time is so brief that the fish retains its shape, texture, moistness and flavour, providing it is not overcooked. So be very careful with your timing. It's a good idea to open the oven door every now and again and test the fish since it may be cooked before the recipe suggests. Always add standing time once the fish has been removed from the oven to allow the fish to finish cooking.

Most fish or fish products are available in regular, easily-managed shapes, but sometimes one end can be thinner than the other. In this case be sure to place the thinnest part of the fish towards the centre of the plate and the thickest to the outside, and shield very thin fillets with a small piece of aluminium foil.

Always cover the fish – microwave cling film is ideal – and ensure that the cover has a vent to allow steam to escape. (In the case of microwave cling film simply pierce 2 or 3 holes.)

If whole fish is being cooked, then make several incisions across the skin to prevent it from bursting.

Apply the golden rule to good microwave cooking: turn and reposition the fish during cooking.

Shellfish also cooks wonderfully in the microwave oven, but it too will suffer badly if overcooked. The flesh tends to toughen. The larger varieties such as lobster and crab are best cooked conventionally. The cooked flesh can then be used in a 'made-up' dish such as Lobster Thermidor or Potted Crab.

KEDGEREE

SERVES 4

1½ lb (750 g) smoked
   haddock
1 oz (25 g) butter
4 oz (100 g) onion, peeled
   and finely diced
1 clove garlic, peeled and
   crushed
½ teaspoon parsley, chopped
12 oz (350 g) long grain rice
1 tablespoon curry powder
   (more if you dare)
1¼ pints (750 ml) fish or
   chicken stock, hot
2 oz (50 g) butter
3 hard-boiled eggs, roughly
   chopped
Salt and freshly ground
   black pepper
1 teaspoon chopped parsley

1. Place the smoked haddock in a shallow dish, cover and cook on HIGH for 7 to 9 minutes. Alter the position of the fish after 4 minutes to ensure even cooking. Place the fish to one side.

2. Melt the butter in a medium bowl on HIGH for 1 minute. Add the onion, garlic and parsley. Cook on HIGH for 3 minutes, then add the rice and cook for a further 2 minutes.

3. Sprinkle on the curry powder, mix in well and add the hot stock. Cover and cook on HIGH for 12 minutes, then leave to stand for a further 6 to 8 minutes to complete the cooking.

4. Flake the fish, ensuring all bones and skin are removed, and stir it into the rice. Add the butter and two-thirds of the boiled egg. Using a fork, gently mix the ingredients together.

5. Check and adjust the seasoning if necessary. Garnish with the remainder of the egg and a little chopped parsley.

POACHED HADDOCK WITH VERMOUTH AND DILL SAUCE

This simple dish produces an unusually flavoured sauce, light yet substantial with a mysterious backbite. It should have your guests guessing for ages.

SERVES 4

4 × 6-oz (175-g) haddock
  steaks
4 sprigs of dill
2 fl oz (50 ml) vermouth
1 fl oz (25 ml) dry white
  wine
1 bay leaf
4 fl oz (120 ml) plain yoghurt
1 fl oz (25 ml) double cream
Salt and freshly ground
  black pepper

1. Arrange the fish in a shallow dish with the thinnest parts to the centre. Top each steak with a sprig of dill.

2. Pour over the vermouth and white wine and add the bay leaf.

3. Cover and cook on HIGH for 6 to 8 minutes. Turn over and rearrange after 4 minutes.

4. Carefully remove the fish from the cooking liquid and place to one side.

5. Add the yoghurt and cream to the liquid, cover and cook on HIGH for 3 minutes. Do not allow to boil. Season lightly with salt and freshly ground black pepper.

6. Return the fish to the sauce and cook on HIGH for a further 2 minutes.

7. Leave to stand, covered, for 2 minutes. Remove the bay leaf and serve.

Mariners' Terrine with Lemon Yoghurt Dressing

SERVES 4

1 teaspoon vegetable oil
2 oz (50 g) vine leaves,
blanched and dried
12 oz (350 g) salmon fillet,
skinned
1 egg white
6 fl oz (175 ml) double cream
1 teaspoon fresh chopped
dill
1 tablespoon snipped chives
Juice of ½ lemon
½ teaspoon paprika
Salt and freshly ground
black pepper

For the dressing:
8 fl oz (250 ml) plain yoghurt
Juice of 1 lemon
½ teaspoon finely snipped
chives
Freshly ground black pepper

4 sprigs of dill or fennel

1. Lightly grease a 2-pint (1.2-l) terrine mould with oil, line it with the vine leaves and place in the refrigerator to chill.

2. Place the salmon in a food processor and purée until smooth. Add the egg white and mix for 2 to 3 minutes, then add the cream. Mix carefully, watching to ensure that the mixture does not curdle, until nearly doubled in volume.

3. Carefully mix in the dill, chives, lemon juice and paprika and season to taste.

4. Transfer the mixture into the prepared mould, making sure the surface is smooth.

5. Cover the terrine with a sheet of greaseproof paper and cook on MEDIUM for about 6 minutes. (Once cooked it should feel firm but springy.) Leave, covered, for 3 minutes to stand.

6. Carefully remove the juices by placing a wire tray over the surface of the terrine and turning upside down thus enabling the juices to flow and the terrine to remain.

7. Once cool, remove from the mould and leave in the refrigerator to chill until ready to serve.

8. Prepare the dressing by simply mixing together the yoghurt, lemon juice and chives. Season with black pepper to taste.

9. Place a slice of terrine on to a plate flooded with the dressing and highlight with a sprig of dill or fennel.

DARNE OF SALMON WITH TARRAGON AND GARLIC BUTTER

This dish capitalises on the meaty texture of salmon in the cut known as 'darne'. This simply means a cut from a round fish through the bone.

The butter can be made well in advance, rolled in greaseproof paper and frozen. Simply take it out of the freezer when required and cut a thick slice ready to serve.

SERVES 4

4 × 6-oz (175-g) salmon
   darne
2 oz (50 g) flour
4 oz (100 g) butter, melted
Salt and freshly ground
   black pepper

For the butter:
8 oz (225 g) unsalted butter
2–3 cloves garlic, peeled and
   crushed
1 tablespoon fresh tarragon,
   chopped or 1 teaspoon
   dried tarragon
A pinch of paprika
Juice of 1 lemon

4 thick slices of lemon
4 sprigs of fresh tarragon

1. Pre-heat a large browning dish, according to the manufacturer's instructions.

2. Lightly flour the salmon steaks, shake off the surplus and then coat them in the melted butter. Season with salt and freshly ground black pepper.

3. Place on to the pre-heated browning dish and cook on HIGH for 6 to 8 minutes. Turn over and rearrange their position after 5 minutes. (The salmon is cooked once the small bone in the centre of the darne is easily removed with a fork.)

4. Mix together all the ingredients for the butter and then roll it on a clean surface into a sausage shape.

5. Place the butter in the centre of a sheet of greaseproof paper. Bring the edges of the paper together lengthways to wrap up the butter and twist the ends. Place in the freezer until firm.

6. Place a thick slice of butter on each hot salmon darne and a thick slice of lemon with a sprig of fresh tarragon as garnish.

POACHED TURBOT WITH MALTAISE SAUCE

SERVES 4

8 × 4-oz (100-g) fillets of
   turbot, skinned
Salt and freshly ground
   black pepper
1 oz (25 g) butter
2 fl oz (50 ml) dry white
   wine
1 bay leaf
6 black peppercorns
3 sprigs of parsley

For the sauce:
1 tablespoon wine vinegar
1 teaspoon crushed black
   peppercorns
5 oz (150 g) unsalted butter
2 egg yolks
Juice of 2 blood oranges (if
   not available use small
   Jaffas)
Zest of 1 blood orange, cut
   into thin strips and
   blanched
Salt and freshly ground
   black pepper

4 slices of blood orange
4 sprigs of parsley

1. Season each fillet and roll up to form a barrel shape. Grease a shallow dish with the butter and lay the fillets in the dish.

2. Pour over the wine, add the bay leaf, peppercorns and parsley, cover and place in a cool place.

3. To make the sauce, place the wine vinegar and peppercorns in a large bowl and cook on HIGH for 2 to 3 minutes (enough time to reduce the liquid by half). Leave to cool.

4. In a separate bowl melt the butter on HIGH for 1½ minutes.

5. Add the egg yolks to the vinegar and peppercorns, mix well and cook on MEDIUM for 30 seconds.

6. Place the fish in the microwave and cook, covered, on HIGH for 6 to 8 minutes, rearranging at least once during cooking.

7. Whilst the fish is cooking, slowly and forcefully beat in the butter to the egg yolks (do this with great care or it may curdle).

8. Once all the butter is added then add and mix in the orange juice and then strain the sauce. Add the strips of orange zest, then check and adjust the seasoning if necessary.

9. Remove the fish from the oven, place it in a clean serving dish and garnish with slices of blood orange and sprigs of parsley. Serve the sauce separately.

MONKFISH IN TOMATO AND OREGANO SAUCE

SERVES 4

1 fl oz (25 ml) olive oil
4 oz (100 g) shallots, finely
  chopped
2 cloves garlic, peeled and
  crushed
1 tablespoon oregano, fresh
  if possible, or 1 teaspoon
  dried
8 tomatoes, skinned,
  deseeded and chopped
1 tablespoon tomato purée
1 bay leaf
1 glass dry white wine
1 lb (450 g) monkfish fillet,
  cut into scampi-sized
  pieces
Salt and freshly ground
  black pepper
A pinch of sugar
2 drops tabasco sauce
3 drops Worcestershire
  sauce

1. Heat the oil in a large bowl on HIGH for 1 minute. Add the shallots and garlic and cook on HIGH for 2 minutes.

2. Add the oregano and chopped tomatoes. Mix in the tomato purée, stir well and cook on HIGH for 2 minutes.

3. Add the bay leaf and dry white wine. Mix well and add the monkfish. Cook on HIGH for 4 to 6 minutes until the fish is cooked.

4. Season lightly with salt and freshly ground black pepper, a pinch of sugar and the tabasco and Worcestershire sauce. Remove the bay leaf.

5. Serve with a crisp green salad.

Paupiettes of Sole in Oakvat Cider

SERVES 4

4 small sole, filleted
4 oz (100 g) prawns, cooked
  and peeled
2 oz (50 g) shallots, finely
  chopped
1 teaspoon chopped parsley
½ pint (300 ml) dry cider
2 oz (50 g) unsalted butter,
  cut into small cubes and
  chilled
2 tablespoons cream or plain
  yoghurt
Salt and freshly ground
  black pepper

1. Lay the fillets flat, season them very lightly with salt and freshly ground black pepper. Place a few prawns in the centre and roll the fillet up from the tail end incorporating the prawns on the inside.

2. Sprinkle the finely chopped onions and parsley over the bottom of a shallow dish and lay the paupiettes of sole on top. Add the cider.

3. Microwave on HIGH for about 6 to 8 minutes until the fish is just cooked.

4. Carefully drain off the cooking liquid into a conventional pan and place on the stove over a full heat. Cover the fish and keep it warm. Allow the liquid in the pan to reduce by half.

5. Draw the pan away from the heat and gently beat in the small cubes of butter, one piece at a time. This will slightly thicken the liquid. Add the cream or yoghurt. Taste and adjust the seasoning if necessary. Do not re-boil the sauce.

6. Pour the sauce over the fish and serve immediately.

HERRINGS WITH DIJON MUSTARD SAUCE

SERVES 4

2 oz (50 g) butter
2 oz (50 g) flour
¾ pint (450 ml) milk
2 tablespoons Dijon mustard
Juice of ½ lemon
Salt and freshly ground
    black pepper
1 tablespoon chopped
    parsley
2 tablespoons single cream
1 egg yolk
4 large herrings, gutted and
    heads removed
2 oz (50 g) butter

1. Melt the butter in a large bowl on HIGH for 1 minute. Add the flour and mix in well to make a roux. Cook on HIGH for 1 minute. Gradually add the milk, stirring in, then cook on HIGH for 3 to 4 minutes, stirring frequently.

2. Add the mustard and lemon juice to the sauce and season to taste. Mix in the parsley, cream and egg yolk. Cover and leave to stand.

3. Arrange the herrings in a shallow serving dish and spread with 2 oz (50 g) of butter. Season lightly with salt and freshly ground black pepper. Cover with microwave cling film and cook on HIGH for 2 to 3 minutes. Turn the herrings over, cover and cook for a further 2 to 3 minutes until cooked. Remove from the oven and leave to stand for 1 minute. Serve the sauce separately or poured over the herrings.

SKATE WITH BLACK BUTTER AND LEMON SAUCE

SERVES 4

4 skate wings
Salt and freshly ground
    black pepper
1 glass white wine
2 fl oz (50 ml) water
Juice of ½ lemon
½ bay leaf
4 black peppercorns
1 oz (25 g) parsley stalks

1. Season the skate wings with salt and freshly ground black pepper and place in a shallow dish with the wine and water, the juice of ½ lemon, the bay leaf, peppercorns and parsley stalks. Cover and cook on HIGH for 8 to 9 minutes until cooked. Remove the fish to a clean warmed dry serving dish and cover.

6 oz (175 g) unsalted butter
1 teaspoon chopped parsley
Juice of ½ lemon

2. Place the butter in a medium bowl, cover and cook on HIGH for 5 to 6 minutes. Add the chopped parsley and remaining lemon juice. Pour over the skate and serve.

FRICASSÉE OF SHELLFISH WITH SAFFRON RICE

SERVES 4

1 oz (25 g) butter
3 oz (75 g) onion, peeled and
  finely diced
4 oz (100 g) scallops,
  quartered
3 oz (75 g) scampi
3 oz (75 g) mushrooms,
  sliced
1 tablespoon chopped
  parsley
½ teaspoon French mustard
4 fl oz (120 ml) white wine
2 oz (50 g) shelled prawns
1 egg yolk, lightly beaten
2 fl oz (50 ml) cream or plain
  yoghurt
Salt and freshly ground
  black pepper

4 portions saffron rice

1. Place the butter in a large bowl and melt on HIGH for 45 seconds. Add the onions and cook for 1 minute.

2. Add the scallops, scampi, mushrooms and parsley and cook on HIGH for 3 to 4 minutes.

3. Mix in the French mustard, wine and prawns and cook on HIGH for 2 to 3 minutes.

4. Mix together the egg yolk and cream or yoghurt. Add to the fish, gently stir to blend through and cook on HIGH for 1 minute. Season to taste with salt and freshly ground black pepper.

5. Serve with saffron rice.

MOULES FORESTIÈRE

SERVES 4

4 pints (2.25 l) mussels
2 oz (50 g) butter
4 oz (100 g) onion, peeled
and finely chopped
4 oz (100 g) bacon, rind
removed and diced
6 oz (175 g) mushrooms,
sliced
2 cloves garlic, peeled and
crushed
2 tablespoons chopped
parsley
12 fl oz (350 ml) dry white
wine
Juice of ½ lemon
1 bay leaf
Salt and freshly ground
black pepper

1. Check to make sure that the mussels are fresh and alive. Discard any shells which are not tightly closed.

2. Brush and wash the shells well. Remove any barnacles and weeds. Use a sharp knife to remove the beards. Rinse the shells in running cold water until all the grit has gone. Put to one side.

3. Place the butter in a bowl large enough to hold the mussels. Melt on HIGH for 1 minute. Add the onion, bacon, mushrooms and garlic. Cover and cook on HIGH for 4 to 5 minutes.

4. Add the parsley, wine, lemon juice and bay leaf, cover and cook on HIGH for 2 minutes.

5. Place the mussels in the bowl. Cook on HIGH, covered, for 5 to 6 minutes or until all the shells are open. Toss the mussels at least twice during cooking. Season lightly with salt and freshly ground black pepper.

6. Pile the mussels on to large, wide soup plates and pour the cooking liquid over them.

7. Serve with plenty of warm French bread.

Trout with Capers and Nut Brown Butter

SERVES 4

2 oz (50 g) butter
4 trout, gutted, washed and
    dried
Salt and freshly ground
    black pepper
5 oz (150 g) unsalted butter
3 tablespoons capers
1 teaspoon chopped parsley
Juice of ½ lemon
4 slices of lemon
½ teaspoon chopped parsley

1. Place the 2 oz (50 g) of butter in a shallow dish and microwave on HIGH for 1 minute. Add the trout, season with salt and pepper and cook on HIGH for 8 to 10 minutes. Cover and leave to stand for 5 minutes before serving. (Check to make sure they are cooked through.)

2. Place the 5 oz (125 g) of butter in a small bowl, cover and cook on HIGH for 5 to 6 minutes. Add the capers, parsley and lemon juice and cook for a further 1 minute.

3. Pour the sauce over the trout. Garnish with slices of lemon and freshly chopped parsley.

King Prawns in Café de Paris Butter

This is real seduction stuff. Remember to have a small bowl of rose scented warm water and a napkin handy in order to clean up afterwards.

SERVES 4

6 oz (175 g) butter
2 cloves garlic, peeled and
    crushed
2 oz (50 g) shallots, very
    finely diced
1 lb (450 g) whole king
    prawns (or more if you
    fancy)
1 tablespoon paprika
1 tablespoon chopped
    parsley
Freshly ground black pepper
Lots of warm garlic bread

1. Melt the butter in a large bowl on HIGH for 1 minute. Add the garlic and shallots. Cook on HIGH for 2 minutes.

2. Add the prawns, paprika and parsley. Season with the black pepper and cook on HIGH for 4 to 5 minutes until cooked. (Do make sure they are cooked right through.)

3. Serve immediately with garlic-oozing bread and stay indoors for two days!

SCALLOPS SMITAINE

SERVES 4

8 large shelled scallops
2 oz (50 g) butter
2 oz (50 g) shallots, finely
   chopped
2 oz (50 g) bacon, rind
   removed and finely diced
2 oz (50 g) mushrooms,
   finely chopped
1 clove garlic, peeled and
   crushed
2 tomatoes, skinned,
   deseeded and finely diced
1 glass vodka
½ glass white wine
¼ pint (150 ml) double
   cream
Salt and freshly ground
   black pepper
4 scallop shells, edges piped
   with potato and browned
1 teaspoon chopped parsley
1 teaspoon paprika
4 sprigs of parsley

1. Halve the scallops and pierce the coral twice with a fork (to prevent them from bursting).

2. Melt the butter in a medium bowl on HIGH for 45 seconds. Add the shallots and bacon and cook on HIGH for 2 minutes. Add the mushrooms, garlic and tomatoes, mix well and cook on HIGH for 3 minutes.

3. Add the vodka and white wine and mix well. Add the scallops, cover and cook on HIGH for 2 minutes. (The scallops should be opaque.)

4. Stir in the cream and season lightly with salt and freshly ground black pepper. Cover and cook on HIGH for 2 minutes.

5. Transfer into the prepared shells and garnish with a little chopped parsley and a dash of paprika over the sauce and a little sprig of parsley on the base of the shell.

LOBSTER THERMIDOR

SERVES 2

1½ lb (750 g) lobster, boiled
2 oz (50 g) butter
2 oz (50 g) shallots, finely
    chopped
1 clove garlic, peeled and
    crushed
1 teaspoon chopped parsley
1 teaspoon French mustard
1 glass white wine
½ glass brandy
Juice of ½ lemon
¼ pint (150 ml) double
    cream
Salt and freshly ground
    black pepper
1 tablespoon grated
    Parmesan cheese
2 egg yolks
2 halves of lemon topped
    with sprigs of parsley

1. Cut the lobster in half lengthways and detach the claws from the body. Remove the fleshy tail meat, cut into large pieces and put to one side. Remove and discard the innards within the main lobster body section and rinse the shells well. Turn upside down to enable the moisture to drain off.

2. Crack the claws and remove the flesh from the inside. (This is best done using a pick or fork.) Cut it into large pieces and add to the tail meat.

3. Melt the butter in a large bowl on HIGH for 1 minute and add the chopped shallots, crushed garlic and chopped parsley. Cook on HIGH for a further 4 minutes.

4. Add the French mustard, white wine, brandy and lemon juice. Cook on HIGH for 2 minutes, then add the cream and cook on HIGH for a further 4 to 5 minutes until the liquid has reached sauce consistency. Season lightly with salt, freshly ground black pepper and Parmesan cheese.

5. Place the lobster meat into the sauce, cover and cook on HIGH for 1 to 2 minutes until hot.

6. Divide into the two shells, being sure not to use all of the sauce.

7. Add the egg yolks to the remaining sauce, mix thoroughly and pour over the top of the lobster.

8. Place the shells under a pre-heated grill for just a few moments to allow the sauce to become golden brown.

9. Serve garnished with lemon halves and parsley.

POTTED CRAB

This recipe is so old even Delia Smith hasn't used it yet. Its also very easy.

SERVES 4

2 oz (50 g) butter
12 oz (350 g) crab meat,
  white and brown, cooked
3 fl oz (85 ml) double cream
Juice of ½ lemon
2 drops tabasco sauce (more
  if you dare)
Salt and freshly ground
  black pepper
1 teaspoon chopped parsley
2 oz (50 g) butter, to cover
4 crab legs
4 sprigs of fennel leaves or
  parsley

1. Melt 2 oz (50 g) of butter in a large bowl on HIGH for 45 seconds. Add the crab meat, mix together and cook on MEDIUM for 4 minutes. Stir frequently and check to ensure that the mixture is thoroughly heated.

2. Add the cream, lemon juice and tabasco and mix well. Cook on MEDIUM for 4 to 5 minutes until the mixture thickens slightly.

3. Season lightly with salt and freshly ground black pepper and mix in the chopped parsley.

4. Spoon the mixture into 4 ramekin dishes and allow to cool.

5. Place the 2 oz (50 g) of butter in a small bowl and melt on HIGH for 1 minute. Leave to cool slightly in order to allow the solids to form at the base of the bowl, and gently spoon the clarified butter over the top of each ramekin.

6. Place in the refrigerator to cool and set.

7. Serve garnished with crab legs and fennel. It tastes delicious served with fresh brown bread.

MEAT, POULTRY AND GAME

In view of the fact that meat varies so much in shape, size and density, it is difficult to give a specific indication of cooking time. So, when selecting meat to be roasted, choose a joint which has a regular compact shape to help ensure even cooking.

It is advisable to trim away any excess fat prior to cooking as well as using a roasting rack, which will allow the fat to drain away and not be reabsorbed into the meat.

One drawback of microwaving small joints of meat is that they tend to look pale and unappetising when cooked. You can improve their appearance by browning the surface under a grill or lightly frying the joint either before or after cooking in the microwave. You may come across alternative ways of browning meat, such as using microwave browning powder, or coating the meat in soy sauce or coloured spices, but these seem highly suspicious to me. I consider it important to achieve the correct appearance as traditionally as possible, and if not, then I won't use the microwave for that particular dish.

One last thing to remember is that however magical a microwave oven is it cannot tenderise the cheap, tougher cuts of meat.

The first rule when cooking poultry, no matter what the method, is to ensure that it is completely and thoroughly cooked. There is no such thing as a 'medium to rare' chicken breast in any good cook's vocabulary. So if you are cooking poultry for the first time in a microwave oven and using the tried and tested 'trial and error' method, check before you serve that all the pieces are cooked. The microwave, unlike a conventional oven, generates less power in the centre of the oven, thus foods will cook unevenly if not repositioned. You could, therefore, find that parts of the chicken are cooked and other parts only half cooked.

All forms of poultry will cook well in a microwave oven. The tender flesh lends itself to this form of cooking, but do be realistic. The oven capacity will determine the size of the bird that can be cooked, so be sure that it will fit inside before you buy the huge turkey and stagger all the way home with it under your arm.

Whole birds are best cooked in a roasting bag which should be loosely tied with string or an elastic band. Generally speaking, you will get the best results by cooking for a longer cooking time at a lower power level.

If, however, you decide to cook using the high power, then shield the legs with narrow strips of foil. This will help prevent them from overcooking and drying out. Allow a standing time for the internal temperature to rise.

When cooking chicken pieces, identify the thinnest or narrowest parts of the joint, place them to the centre of the plate and shield them with a little foil. Turn and reposition the joints during cooking to ensure even cooking. Should you require the joints to be browned then use a browning dish for the best effect.

For very tender pieces such as breasts or supremes of chicken which tend to be boneless it is advisable to remove the skin (if you do not, then colour in a browning dish first and cook skin side down for the first half of the cooking process) and allow plenty of space between portions. Once again it is important to turn and reposition the pieces during cooking.

As microwaves are attracted to moisture it goes without saying that a casserole is an ideal dish to cook. Be aware of timing. Different types of food do not cook in the same length of time, so begin the dish by cooking vegetables etc., and back-time the point at which you should add the meat according to how tender it is.

Don't overcrowd the dish. Allow enough space in order to move the ingredients around every now and again.

Avoid very tough types of game. The microwave is not the best form of cooking for these. And take note of the defrosting guidelines for poultry and game on page 26.

PAUPIETTES OF BEEF

SERVES 4

2 oz (50 g) butter
2 oz (50 g) shallots, finely chopped
1 clove garlic, peeled and crushed
2 oz (50 g) mushrooms, finely chopped
1 teaspoon chopped parsley
4 oz (100 g) fresh white breadcrumbs
A pinch of mixed herbs
1 egg, beaten
Salt and freshly ground black pepper
1½ lb (750 g) topside beef, cut into 8 thin slices
2 oz (50 g) flour
1 oz (25 g) butter
1 tablespoon olive or vegetable oil
4 oz (100 g) onions, peeled and sliced
1 oz (25 g) flour
1 tablespoon tomato purée
2–3 drops of Worcestershire sauce
1 glass red wine
½ pint (300 ml) beef stock, hot
1 bouquet garni

1. Melt the butter in a large bowl on HIGH for 1 minute. Add the shallots, garlic, mushrooms and parsley. Cover and cook on HIGH for 5 minutes, stirring occasionally.

2. Remove from the oven and add the breadcrumbs, herbs and egg. Season with salt and freshly ground black pepper and mix together thoroughly.

3. Place the slices of beef inside a plastic bag and beat it flat. Remove the beef from the bag and cover each piece with the stuffing. Roll the meat in order to enclose the stuffing thus creating the 'paupiette'. Secure with string or a wooden cocktail stick.

4. Coat each paupiette in flour and gently shake off the surplus. (Do this carefully otherwise the stuffing may fall out!)

5. Melt the butter and oil together in a shallow ovenproof casserole dish on HIGH for 1 minute. Add the paupiettes, roll them to coat them in fat, then cover and microwave on HIGH for 6 to 7 minutes. Turn the meat frequently.

6. Place the paupiettes on to a clean plate and add the onions to the hot dish. Cover and cook on HIGH for 4 minutes. Mix in the flour and tomato purée. Pour on the Worcestershire sauce, red wine and gradually mix in the hot stock. Add the bouquet garni and immerse the paupiettes in the sauce.

7. Cover and cook on HIGH for 8 minutes then reduce the setting to LOW and cook for 25 to 30 minutes until the paupiettes are tender. Remove the string or cocktail sticks and leave the dish to stand, well covered, for 8 minutes before serving. Remember to remove the bouquet garni.

FILLET OF BEEF STROGANOFF

This is a really luxurious dish and can be a little expensive. It is possible to use cheaper cuts of meat, such as sirloin, although not much cheaper. But it really does need a tender cut in order to get the best results. It's lovely with a bowl of basmati rice.

SERVES 4

1 teaspoon olive oil
1 lb (450 g) beef fillet, trimmed and cut into 2- × ½-in (5- × 1-cm) strips
Salt and freshly ground black pepper
1 clove garlic, peeled and crushed
3 oz (75 g) shallots, finely chopped
4 oz (100 g) mushrooms, sliced
1 teaspoon tarragon, chopped
1 bay leaf
1 glass white wine
1 glass brandy
1 teaspoon French mustard
6 fl oz (175 ml) double cream
2 oz (50 g) gherkins, thinly sliced lengthways

1. Heat a browning dish according to the manufacturer's instructions and add the oil. Add the beef fillet, season lightly with salt and freshly ground black pepper and mix well. Cook on HIGH for 2 minutes, then add the garlic, shallots, mushrooms and tarragon. Cover and cook on HIGH for 3 minutes, stirring frequently.

2. Add the bay leaf, white wine and brandy. Mix in the French mustard and cream.

3. Check and adjust the seasoning if necessary. Add the sliced gherkins and cook on HIGH for 3 minutes until the stroganoff has formed a sauce consistency. Remove the bay leaf and serve with plain boiled rice.

Salmon and Prawn Mousse with Lemon
and Lime Salad (*page 42*)

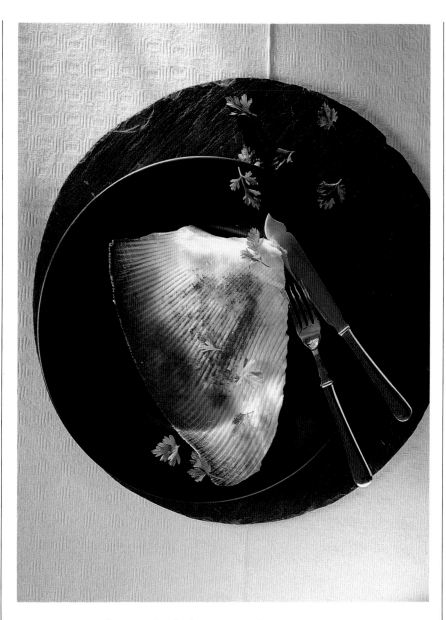

Skate with Black Butter and Lemon Sauce
(*page 54*)

Noisettes of Lamb with Garlic and Ginger
(*page 69*) and Harlequin Vegetables
(*page 106*)

Warm Salad of Duckling with Cherry and
Mangetout Salad (*page 82*)

Spaghetti Alle Vongole (*page 90*)

Dark Chocolate Mousse with White
Chocolate Sauce (*page 110*)

Muesli Slices (*page 125*) and Cherry and
Almond Biscuits (*page 124*)

Dark Chocolate Fudge Fingers (*page 126*)
and Soda Bread (*page 133*)

BEEF, KIDNEY AND MUSHROOM PUDDING

This 'winter special' dish should be eaten directly after being cooked in order to derive the best from the recipe.

SERVES 4

1 glass red wine
4 oz (100 g) onions, peeled
  and chopped
1 bay leaf
½ teaspoon tarragon
½ teaspoon thyme
1 lb (450 g) braising steak,
  cut into 1-in (2.5-cm)
  cubes
1 oz (25 g) flour
4 oz (100 g) carrots, peeled
  and finely diced
6 oz (175 g) ox kidney, core
  removed and diced
Salt and freshly ground
  black pepper
6 oz (175 g) button
  mushrooms, whole if
  small or quartered if large
8 oz (225 g) self-raising flour
A pinch of salt
4 oz (100 g) shredded suet
6–8 fl oz (175–250 ml) cold
  water

1. Place the wine and onion with the herbs in a large bowl and cook on HIGH for 3 minutes.

2. Add the beef and cook on HIGH for 2 minutes. Mix in the flour and cook, covered, on HIGH for 12 minutes, stirring frequently.

3. Add the carrots and kidney, cover and cook on LOW for 35 to 40 minutes until the meat is tender.

4. Season lightly with salt and freshly ground black pepper. Add the mushrooms and remove the bay leaf.

5. Make the pastry by mixing together the flour, salt and suet. Slowly add the water, mixing all the time, until it forms a dough. Divide into one-third and two-thirds. Roll out the larger piece and line a 2-pint (1.2-l) pudding basin. Roll the remaining third for the lid and put to one side.

6. Transfer the meat mixture into the mould. Wet the edges of the pastry with cold water and place on the pastry lid. Cover the pudding with microwave cling film, venting one corner, and cook on HIGH for 9 to 11 minutes.

7. Remove the microwave cling film and serve.

BRAISED BURGUNDY BEEF

SERVES 4

4 oz (100 g) back bacon, rind
   removed and diced
1½ lb (750 g) beef, good
   quality cut such as sirloin,
   rump or topside, cubed
2 cloves garlic, peeled and
   crushed
1 teaspoon chopped parsley
4 oz (100 g) button onions
Salt and freshly ground
   black pepper
A pinch of thyme
1 oz (25 g) flour
2 tomatoes, skinned,
   deseeded and finely
   chopped
1 tablespoon tomato purée
8 fl oz (250 ml) red wine
2 fl oz (50 ml) beef stock, hot
4 oz (100 g) button
   mushrooms

1. Place the bacon in a large earthenware casserole and cook on HIGH for 4 minutes.

2. Add the pieces of beef, garlic, parsley and button onions. Season lightly with salt, freshly ground black pepper and thyme. Cook on HIGH for 2 minutes.

3. Add the flour, tomatoes and tomato purée and mix in well. Gradually add the wine and the hot beef stock.

4. Cover and cook on HIGH for 6 minutes. Add the mushrooms, reduce the oven to LOW and cook for 45 minutes or until the meat is tender. Stir frequently.

5. Check and adjust the seasoning if necessary.

CHILLI CON CARNE

SERVES 4

1 tablespoon olive or
   vegetable oil
4 oz (100 g) onions, peeled
   and finely diced
1 clove garlic, peeled and
   crushed
2 oz (50 g) green pepper,
   deseeded and finely diced
2 oz (50 g) red pepper,
   deseeded and finely diced
1 lb (450 g) ground beef
4 tomatoes, skinned,
   deseeded and finely diced
1 tablespoon tomato purée
1 teaspoon chilli powder
1 bay leaf
2 fl oz (50 ml) red wine
1 × 8-oz (225-g) can of red
   kidney beans, drained
Salt and freshly ground
   black pepper

1. Heat the oil in a large bowl on HIGH for 1 minute. Add the onion, garlic, green and red peppers, cover and cook on HIGH for 4 minutes. Stir once during cooking.

2. Add the ground beef and mix in well with a wooden spoon. Cover and cook on HIGH for 6 minutes, stirring frequently during cooking.

3. Add the tomatoes, tomato purée, chilli powder, bay leaf and red wine. Cover and cook on HIGH for 25 to 30 minutes (check to satisfy yourself that the meat is cooked to your liking).

4. Add the kidney beans, cover and cook on HIGH for 4 minutes. Check and adjust the seasoning if necessary. (If you like it hotter add a drop or two of tabasco sauce.)

5. Remove the bay leaf and serve with a rice dish.

SCALLOPINES OF VEAL MARSALA

This recipe, which can be used for pork if veal is not available, is ideal for that special occasion and equally useful for a quick snack if scaled down.

SERVES 4

1 lb (450 g) veal fillet, cut into small pieces
2 oz (50 g) streaky bacon, rind removed
Salt and freshly ground black pepper
½ teaspoon sage, chopped
2 oz (50 g) butter
2 oz (50 g) shallots, finely chopped
1 clove garlic, peeled and crushed
½ teaspoon crushed black peppercorns
1 bay leaf
1 glass Marsala
2 fl oz (50 ml) chicken stock, hot
4 fl oz (120 ml) double cream

1. Place the small pieces of veal inside a plastic bag and gently beat them with a heavy flat implement to flatten them out to form small escalopes.

2. Cut the bacon into thin short strips.

3. Season the veal with salt, freshly ground black pepper and sage.

4. Pre-heat a browning dish according to the manufacturer's instructions and add the butter. Add the veal and bacon and cook on HIGH for 1 minute on each side.

5. Add the shallots, garlic, peppercorns and bay leaf. Cover and cook on HIGH for 3 minutes. Pour in the Marsala. Cook on HIGH for 1 minute, then add the chicken stock and cream. Cover and cook on HIGH for 2 minutes until the sauce has thickened.

6. Check and adjust the seasoning if necessary. Remove the bay leaf and serve. It tastes delicious with a crisp green salad and small new baked potatoes.

NOISETTES OF LAMB WITH GARLIC AND GINGER

SERVES 4

6 oz (175 g) butter
1 tablespoon chopped
  parsley
1 clove garlic, peeled and
  crushed
½ oz (15 g) root ginger,
  peeled and finely diced
Juice of ½ lemon
Freshly ground black pepper
8 noisettes or cutlets of lamb
2 cloves garlic, peeled and
  cut into thin strips
1 oz (25 g) root ginger, peeled
  and cut into similar size
  pieces to the garlic
1 tablespoon olive or
  vegetable oil
1 bunch of watercress,
  picked and washed
4 tomatoes, grilled

1. Place the butter in a bowl and soften in the microwave on LOW for 10 seconds. Add the parsley, crushed garlic and diced ginger. Season with lemon juice and black pepper and mix well.

2. Place the butter on to a piece of greaseproof paper and roll the paper around the butter so that it is completely enclosed. Tuck in both ends to force the butter into a cylindrical shape. (It should now have the appearance of a bar of Manx rock.) Place this in the chiller section of the refrigerator.

3. Lightly season the noisettes and make four small incisions with the point of a knife into the meat. Place 2 pieces of garlic and ginger in the incisions.

4. Pre-heat a browning dish according to the manufacturer's instructions and add 1 tablespoon of oil. Place the noisettes in the dish and cook on HIGH for 3 minutes. Turn them over and cook for a further 4 to 5 minutes until cooked to your liking.

5. Serve on a clean dish garnished with a thick slice of the garlic and ginger butter, grilled tomato and watercress.

BRAISED LAMBS' LIVER
OLD ENGLAND FASHION

Lambs' liver for me used to bring back memories of school days. I recall being overfaced with this sad looking piece of offal, overcooked and totally inedible. This recipe is for those whose recall of liver was like mine. It produces a most flavoursome dish entirely different to the endurance cuisine of the late 50s. (There I go again, giving my age away.)

SERVES 4

1 lb (450 g) lambs' liver, washed
2 oz (50 g) flour
Salt and freshly ground black pepper
2 oz (50 g) butter
6 oz (175 g) onions, peeled and sliced
2 oz (50 g) streaky bacon, rind removed and diced
4 oz (100 g) carrots, peeled and sliced
2 oz (50 g) leeks, washed and sliced
2 oz (50 g) celery, washed and sliced
1½ oz (40 g) flour
1 tablespoon tomato purée
½ pint (300 ml) beef stock, hot
¼ pint (150 ml) brown ale
1 bouquet garni

1. Remove and discard any inedible membranes from the liver.

2. Cut the liver into ½-in (1-cm) thick slices and coat in flour. Shake off the surplus. Season lightly with salt and freshly ground black pepper.

3. Melt the butter in a wide bottomed deep pan on a conventional stove. When hot, add the liver, allowing one side to seal, then turn over the liver to seal the other side. Remove from the pan into a deep earthenware casserole dish.

4. Place onion, bacon, carrots, leek and celery in the hot buttered pan and allow to cook gently on the conventional stove. Stir continuously until the onion has softened.

5. Sprinkle on the flour and mix in well, add the tomato purée and gradually mix in the hot beef stock and brown ale.

6. Season lightly with salt and freshly ground black pepper. Add the bouquet garni.

7. Pour the sauce over the liver, cover and cook on HIGH for 16 to 18 minutes.

8. Check and adjust the seasoning if necessary.

9. Remove the bouquet garni and serve.

SPARE RIBS CHINOISE

SERVES 4

2 cloves garlic, peeled and
  chopped
1 glass red wine
4 oz (100 g) onions, peeled
  and sliced
2 tablespoons redcurrant
  jelly
2 tablespoons honey
2 drops tabasco sauce
3 drops Worcestershire
  sauce
1 tablespoon red wine
  vinegar
2 tablespoons soy sauce
Salt and freshly ground
  black pepper
1½ lb (750 g) pork spare ribs
1 heaped tablespoon
  cornflour, dissolved in a
  little cold water

1. Mix together all the ingredients except the salt and pepper, pork ribs and cornflour.

2. Lightly season the ribs with salt and freshly ground black pepper and immerse them in the marinade. Place in the refrigerator and leave to marinate for 4 hours.

3. Remove the ribs from the marinade and lay in a single layer in a shallow earthenware dish. Season lightly with salt and freshly ground black pepper and cover with kitchen paper. Cook on HIGH for 4 minutes. Reposition the ribs and cook on MEDIUM for 20 to 25 minutes until the flesh on the ribs is tender. It is necessary to reposition the ribs at least once during cooking.

4. Add the cornflour mixture to the marinade. Mix in well. Pour the marinade over the ribs and cook on HIGH for 6 to 8 minutes until the ribs are coated with a thick sauce. Reposition the ribs during cooking.

GAMMON STEAKS WITH ROSEMARY AND CIDER SAUCE

SERVES 4

4 × 6-oz (175-g) gammon
  steaks
2 eating apples, peeled, cored
  and sliced
2 oz (50 g) butter, melted
4 sprigs of rosemary
½ pint (300 ml) dry cider
3 tablespoons plain yoghurt
Salt and freshly ground
  black pepper
4 sprigs of rosemary

1. Remove the rind and excess fat from the gammon and lay the steaks in a shallow earthenware casserole dish.

2. Place the apple slices over the gammon, brush with the melted butter and lay 4 sprigs of rosemary, 1 on each steak.

3. Pour the cider over the steaks, cover and cook on HIGH for 5 minutes. Turn and reposition the dish after 3 minutes.

4. Carefully drain off the cooking liquid into a small bowl. Cover the steaks and leave to stand for 4 minutes.

5. Place the cooking liquid in the microwave and cook on HIGH for 1 minute. Remove from the oven and gradually add the yoghurt.

6. Check and adjust the seasoning if necessary. Strain the sauce over the steaks. Garnish with the fresh sprigs of rosemary.

PORK CHOPS IN SOURED CREAM AND PAPRIKA SAUCE

SERVES 4

4 pork chops
Salt and freshly ground
   black pepper
1 tablespoon olive or
   vegetable oil
2 oz (50 g) onion, peeled and
   finely chopped
1 tablespoon paprika
2 oz (50 g) red pepper,
   deseeded and finely diced
2 oz (50 g) eating apples,
   peeled and finely diced
2 oz (50 g) cooked ham,
   finely diced
1 fl oz (25 ml) calvados (or a
   little cider)
Juice of 1 lemon
¼ pint (150 ml) double
   cream
A pinch of paprika
Chopped parsley to garnish

1. Season the chops lightly with salt and freshly ground black pepper.

2. Pre-heat a browning dish according to the manufacturer's instructions. Add the oil and the chops and cook, uncovered, on HIGH for 4 minutes. Reposition and turn them over and cook on HIGH for a further 3 minutes, then transfer them to a clean serving dish.

3. Place the onion, paprika and red pepper into the dish. Cover and cook on HIGH for 3 minutes.

4. Add the apple, ham, calvados, lemon juice and cream, mix well and season lightly.

5. Immerse the chops in the sauce, cover and cook on HIGH for 2 minutes. Reduce the setting to LOW and cook for 16 to 20 minutes until the chops are tender.

6. Leave, well covered, for 5 minutes to stand. Serve garnished with a dusting of paprika and a sprinkling of chopped parsley.

Coq au Vin

This all-time favourite recipe lends itself perfectly to twentieth century interpretation using the microwave.

SERVES 4

1 fl oz (25 ml) vegetable oil
1 × 3½-lb (1.5-kg) chicken,
   cut into 8 pieces
Salt and freshly ground
   black pepper
2 oz (50 g) butter
4 oz (100 g) bacon, rind
   removed and cut into
   small dice
6 oz (175 g) button onions,
   peeled
1 teaspoon chopped parsley
2 cloves garlic, peeled and
   crushed
1 bouquet garni
1¾ pints (1 l) full bodied red
   wine
1 oz (25 g) cornflour,
   dissolved in a little cold
   water
4 heart-shaped slices of
   bread, deep fried and edged
   with chopped parsley

1. Heat the oil in a large frying pan on a conventional cooker. Add the chicken pieces, season lightly with salt and freshly ground black pepper and gently colour the chicken.

2. Melt the butter in a large bowl on HIGH for 1 minute. Add the bacon, button onions, parsley and garlic. Cover and cook on HIGH for 4 minutes.

3. Place the chicken pieces in the bowl, add the bouquet garni and pour over the wine. Cover and cook on HIGH for 25 minutes or until the chicken is thoroughly cooked. Turn and reposition the dish during cooking.

4. Remove the chicken to a clean warm serving dish. Remove and discard the bouquet garni, whisk the cornflour mixture into the sauce and cook on HIGH for 2 minutes.

5. Check and adjust the seasoning if necessary and pour the sauce over the chicken. Garnish with the fried bread and parsley.

CHICKEN MARENGO

This lovely dish is steeped in history. It was created for Napoleon after the Battle of Marengo. His cooks gathered together local produce to create a meal. (I don't believe they possessed a microwave.) Hence the unusual combination of chicken and shellfish, perhaps not so unusual these days.

SERVES 4

1 fl oz (25 ml) vegetable oil
1 × 3-lb (1.5-kg) chicken, cut
   into 8 pieces
Salt and freshly ground
   black pepper
2 oz (50 g) butter
4 oz (100 g) onions, peeled
   and finely chopped
2 cloves garlic, peeled and
   crushed
1 sprig of rosemary
½ teaspoon chopped thyme
1 bay leaf
8 tomatoes, skinned,
   deseeded and finely
   chopped
2 oz (50 g) tomato purée
4 fl oz (120 ml) chicken
   stock, hot
1 glass white wine
4 oz (100 g) small button
   mushrooms, whole
3 oz (75 g) cooked prawns
1 tablespoon chopped
   parsley

1. Place the oil in a frying pan and heat on a conventional stove. Add the chicken pieces, season lightly with salt and freshly ground black pepper and allow the chicken to colour slightly. Remove from the pan and put to one side.

2. Melt the butter in a large bowl and add the onions, garlic, rosemary and thyme and cook on HIGH for 3 minutes.

3. Add the bay leaf, chopped tomatoes and tomato purée and mix in well. Cover and cook on HIGH for 3 minutes.

4. Mix in the hot chicken stock and wine and immerse the chicken into the sauce. Add the button mushrooms, cover and cook on HIGH for 25 minutes or until the chicken is thoroughly cooked. Turn and reposition the dish at least twice during cooking.

5. Check and adjust the seasoning if necessary. (If the tomatoes have made the sauce too 'sharp' for your·taste, add a pinch of sugar. If they are too sweet a little Worcestershire sauce and vinegar will do the trick.) Remove the bay leaf.

6. Transfer into a pre-heated serving dish and garnish with the prawns and chopped parsley.

SAUTÉ OF CHICKEN PROVENÇALE

SERVES 4

1 tablespoon vegetable oil
1 × 3½-lb (1.5-kg) chicken,
   cut into 8 pieces
Salt and freshly ground
   black pepper
2 oz (50 g) butter
6 oz (175 g) onions, peeled
   and very finely chopped
2 cloves garlic, peeled and
   crushed
1 tablespoon basil, chopped
8 ripe tomatoes, skinned,
   deseeded and finely
   chopped
2 oz (50 g) tomato purée
2 fl oz (50 ml) dry white
   wine
2 fl oz (50 ml) chicken stock,
   hot
2 oz (50 g) stoned black
   olives
Basil leaves, washed

1. Heat the oil in a large frying pan on a conventional cooker and add the chicken portions. Season lightly with salt and freshly ground black pepper. Once coloured, remove the chicken from the pan and put to one side.

2. Heat the butter on HIGH for 1 minute in the microwave, add the onions, garlic and basil, cover and cook on HIGH for 3 minutes.

3. Add the chopped tomatoes and tomato purée. Mix well and cook on HIGH for 1 minute.

4. Stir in the dry white wine and the chicken stock and mix thoroughly.

5. Immerse the chicken pieces in the sauce, cover and cook on HIGH for 25 minutes or until the chicken is cooked. (It is essential to ensure that the meat is thoroughly cooked.) Turn and reposition the dish at least twice during cooking.

6. Check and adjust the seasoning if necessary. Serve garnished with the stoned black olives and basil leaves.

MEDALLIONS OF CHICKEN CHINESE STYLE

SERVES 4

4 chicken breasts, skinned
4 oz (100 g) soft brown sugar
2 tablespoons dry sherry
3 tablespoons soy sauce
1 tablespoon wine vinegar
1 tablespoon cornflour,
   dissolved in a little cold
   water
Grated rind of ½ orange
Grated rind of ½ lemon
¼ pint (150 ml) chicken
   stock, hot
½ green pepper, deseeded
   and finely diced
½ red pepper, deseeded and
   finely diced
2 courgettes, halved and
   sliced lengthways
3 oz (75 g) mangetout, cut
   into dice
2 oz (50 g) bean sprouts
4 spring onions, peeled and
   finely diced

1. Lay the chicken breasts on a clean surface and using a sharp knife cut through and across the breasts with the knife held at a slight angle. The medallions should be ¼-in (5-mm) thick pieces.

2. Mix the sugar, dry sherry, soy sauce and vinegar together. Add the cornflour mixture and cook on HIGH for 3 minutes, stirring occasionally.

3. Place the medallions of chicken, orange and lemon rind, chicken stock, green and red pepper and courgettes into the sauce. Cover and cook on HIGH for 15 to 20 minutes. Stir at least 4 times during cooking. It is essential that you check to ensure that the chicken is completely cooked.

4. Add the mangetout and bean sprouts and cook on HIGH, uncovered, for 2 minutes.

5. Sprinkle the raw chopped spring onion over the dish and serve.

SUPREME OF CHICKEN IN WATERCRESS AND MARSALA SAUCE

SERVES 4

2 oz (50 g) butter
2 oz (50 g) carrots, peeled and sliced
2 oz (50 g) onion, peeled and sliced
2 oz (50 g) leeks, washed and sliced
2 oz (50 g) celery, washed and chopped
4 supremes of chicken (breasts), skinned
Salt and freshly ground black pepper
2 sprigs of rosemary
1 bay leaf
1 pint (600 ml) chicken stock, hot
1 glass Marsala, or more if you fancy
1 bunch of watercress, washed, picked, chopped and blanched
Juice of ½ lemon
1 oz (25 g) butter and 1 oz (25 g) flour mixed together to form a paste
1 egg yolk
2 fl oz (50 ml) double cream
8 leaves watercress, washed

1. Melt the butter in a large bowl on HIGH for 1 minute. Add the carrots, onion, leek and celery and cook on HIGH for 2 minutes.

2. Arrange the supremes neatly on the vegetables. Season very lightly with salt and freshly ground pepper. Add the sprigs of rosemary and the bay leaf.

3. Add the hot chicken stock, Marsala and watercress. Cover and cook on HIGH for 12 to 14 minutes until the chicken is thoroughly cooked. Turn and reposition the dish during cooking.

4. Remove the chicken breasts from the cooking liquid and place in a warmed serving dish. Cover and keep warm. Take out and discard the bay leaf and rosemary.

5. Pass the liquid through a food processor, blender or liquidiser into a clean bowl.

6. Add the lemon juice and whisk in the flour and butter paste. Cook on HIGH for 4 to 6 minutes, whisking occasionally.

7. Take a small amount of the hot sauce into a small bowl, add to it the egg yolk and cream mixed together. Stir well and pour this into the rest of the sauce, once again mixing really thoroughly.

8. Check and adjust the seasoning if necessary. Pour over the chicken supremes and garnish with the watercress leaves.

BREAST OF TURKEY IN FENNEL AND MUSHROOM SAUCE

SERVES 4

1 lb (450 g) turkey breast, skinned
2 oz (50 g) butter
4 oz (100 g) fennel, washed and thinly sliced
1 oz (25 g) flour
½ pint (300 ml) chicken stock, hot
4 oz (100 g) button mushrooms, sliced
Juice of ½ lemon
1 fl oz (25 ml) Pernod or Ricard
2 fl oz (50 ml) double cream
Salt and freshly ground black pepper
4 sprigs of fennel leaves to garnish
A pinch of paprika

1. Cut the turkey into 2 × ½-in (5 × 1-cm) strips.

2. Melt the butter on HIGH for 45 seconds, add the turkey and fennel. Cover and cook on HIGH for 4 minutes.

3. Mix in the flour and add the hot chicken stock, stirring constantly. Cover and cook on HIGH for 1½ minutes. Stir and add the mushrooms. Cook on HIGH for a further 1½ minutes.

4. Add the lemon juice, Pernod and cream. Mix in well. Season with salt and freshly ground black pepper.

5. Serve garnished with the fennel leaves and a light dash of paprika.

STIR-FRIED TURKEY

SERVES 4

1 lb (450 g) turkey breast,
skinned
4 oz (100 g) carrots, peeled
and thinly sliced
1 teaspoon chopped parsley
4 oz (100 g) courgettes,
peeled and thinly sliced
8 spring onions, peeled and
chopped
4 oz (100 g) water chestnuts,
sliced
4 oz (100 g) bean sprouts
¼ pint (150 ml) chicken
stock, hot
1 small glass white wine
1 tablespoon soy sauce
2 tablespoons cornflour,
dissolved in a little cold
water
Freshly ground black pepper
and Chinese 5 spice
powder
Chopped parsley to garnish

1. Place the turkey, carrot, parsley and courgettes in a medium bowl and cook on HIGH for 5 minutes. Add the spring onions, water chestnuts and bean sprouts. Mix together, cover and cook on HIGH for 2 minutes. Remove from the microwave and put on one side.

2. In a separate bowl, mix together the chicken stock, white wine, soy sauce, cornflour and seasoning. Whisk until well mixed and cook on HIGH for 2 to 3 minutes, stirring frequently, until the mixture is smooth and has thickened.

3. Mix the sauce and turkey, carrot and courgettes together. Cook for 2 to 3 minutes, garnish with the chopped parsley and serve.

COLLOPS OF TURKEY IN LEEK AND WALNUT YOGHURT

SERVES 4

1 lb (450 g) turkey breast
Salt and freshly ground
  black pepper
2 oz (50 g) butter
8 oz (225 g) leeks, washed
  and sliced
2 oz (50 g) walnuts, chopped
1 tablespoon chopped
  parsley
2 oz (50 g) celery, washed
  and sliced
½ teaspoon oregano,
  chopped
1 oz (25 g) flour
½ pint (300 ml) chicken
  stock, hot
¼ pint (150 ml) plain
  yoghurt
1 egg yolk
2 oz (50 g) chives, washed
  and finely diced
2 oz (50 g) walnut halves
4 sprigs of fresh parsley

1. Remove the skin from the turkey breast and cut the breast into pieces about 1½ in (4 cm) in width the full length of the meat. Lay the lengths flat and cut collops by slicing at a slight angle through the flesh so that each collop is about ½ in (1 cm) thick.

2. Very lightly season them and place them in a roasting bag. Place a rubber band around the ends and cook on HIGH for 6 to 8 minutes. Satisfy yourself that the meat is thoroughly cooked. Remove and put to one side.

3. Melt the butter in a large bowl on HIGH for 1 minute and then add the leeks, walnuts, parsley, celery and oregano. Cover and cook on HIGH for 8 to 10 minutes.

4. Add the flour, mix in well and then gradually add the hot chicken stock. Cook on HIGH for 2 minutes and then whisk. Cook for a further 3 minutes, stirring frequently until the sauce is boiling.

5. Carefully pour any juices from the roasting bag into the sauce and place the collops of turkey in a clean earthenware serving dish.

6. Mix the yoghurt and egg yolk together and add them to the sauce, mixing in thoroughly. Check and adjust the seasoning if necessary. Strain the sauce over the turkey, sprinkle the chopped chives and walnuts over the surface as garnish and decorate with sprigs of fresh parsley.

WARM SALAD OF DUCKLING WITH CHERRY AND MANGETOUT SALAD

SERVES 4

8 leaves frisée lettuce, washed
4 leaves oak leaf lettuce, washed
8 oz (225 g) red cherries, stoned
8 oz (225 g) mangetout
4 breasts duckling, boned
1 tablespoon olive oil or vegetable oil
2 fl oz (50 ml) red wine
1 glass brandy
1 tablespoon tarragon vinegar
Salt and freshly ground black pepper

1. Arrange the lettuce leaves on large plates and garnish with the cherries and mangetout. (This is much nicer if you dress the ingredients first with a little salad dressing such as vinaigrette or an unusual fruit vinegar.) Place in the refrigerator.

2. Pre-heat a browning dish according to the manufacturer's instructions. Add the oil and the duckling breasts, skin side down. Cook on HIGH for 2 minutes, turn over, add the red wine, brandy and vinegar. Season the breasts lightly with salt and freshly ground black pepper. Cook on HIGH for 5 to 6 minutes. Turn once during cooking. Check to ensure the meat is tender and remove from the dish.

3. Place the sauce in the microwave and cook on HIGH for 3 minutes until the sauce has reduced.

4. Cut the breasts at an angle into small collops and place neatly on the salad. Lightly spoon the reduced cooking liquid over the duck and serve immediately.

DUCKLING IN PEPPERCORN AND CLARET SAUCE

SERVES 4

3 oz (75 g) butter
1 clove garlic, peeled and crushed
2 oz (50 g) green peppercorns, or more if you fancy
2 oz (50 g) celery, washed and finely diced
1½ oz (40 g) flour
1 oz (25 g) tomato purée
½ pint (300 ml) beef stock, hot
4 fl oz (120 ml) claret wine
1 bouquet garni
4 × 6-oz (175-g) duckling legs, cut in half
Salt and freshly ground black pepper
2 drops tabasco sauce (optional)
1 oz (25 g) green peppercorns

1. Place 1 oz (25 g) of the butter in a large bowl and melt on HIGH for 45 seconds. Add the garlic, green peppercorns and celery. Cover and cook on HIGH for 6 minutes. Stir half way through cooking.

2. Add the flour and tomato purée and mix in well to form a roux. Cover and cook on HIGH for 3 minutes.

3. Slowly add the hot beef stock, mixing it well into the roux, and then do the same with the claret. Add the bouquet garni.

4. Melt the remainder of the butter in a large frying pan on a conventional oven and cook the duckling just enough to colour the skin golden brown. Remove from the pan and immerse in the sauce.

5. Season lightly with salt, freshly ground black pepper and a little tabasco sauce if liked. Cook on HIGH for 15 minutes and then on LOW for 35 to 45 minutes until the flesh is tender.

6. When cooked, transfer the duckling into a clean serving dish.

7. Check and adjust the seasoning if necessary and if a thinner sauce is preferred add a little more wine or beef stock. Strain the sauce over the duckling and sprinkle the 1 oz (25 g) of green peppercorns over the flesh.

ROAST PHEASANT WITH TARRAGON AND PORT SAUCE

SERVES 4

2 × 1½–1¾-lb (750-g)
pheasants

Salt and freshly ground
black pepper

4 rashers back bacon

1 oz (25 g) butter

3 oz (75 g) leeks, washed,
sliced

3 oz (75 g) carrots, peeled
and diced

1 tablespoon chopped fresh
tarragon or 1 teaspoon
dried

3 tomatoes, skinned,
deseeded and chopped

4 oz (100 g) celery, washed
and sliced

¼ pint (150 ml) port

3 fl oz (85 ml) game stock or
chicken stock, hot

1 tablespoon redcurrant jelly

1 tablespoon cornflour,
dissolved in a little cold
water

2 bunches of watercress,
picked and washed

1. Season the pheasants with salt and freshly ground black pepper and cover the breasts with the bacon. Place them carefully in roasting bags and secure the ends with elastic bands. Place on a shallow dish and prick the top of the bags to allow the steam to escape.

2. Cook on HIGH for 18 minutes. Reposition and turn them over after 9 minutes.

3. Pre-heat a conventional oven to 400°F (200°C), gas mark 6. Remove the birds from the bags and retain any juices that are left. Discard the bacon and place the birds in the conventional oven for 12 to 15 minutes to colour them. (If you don't possess a conventional oven, don't worry. Cover the pheasants with aluminium foil and leave to stand for 10 to 15 minutes. They won't colour, but it will ensure that the birds are thoroughly cooked without drying out.)

4. Place the butter in a large bowl and melt on HIGH for 1 minute. Add the leeks, carrots, tarragon, tomatoes and celery. Cover and cook on HIGH for 8 minutes.

5. Portion the pheasants and place on a clean serving dish. Cover and keep warm. Add the carcass and any juice from the roasting bag and roasting tin to the bowl containing the vegetables.

6. Pour on the port, game or chicken stock and redcurrant jelly. Mix well, cover and cook on HIGH for 4 minutes.

7. Season with salt and freshly ground black pepper and remove any fat from the surface of the sauce by floating absorbent paper over the top.

8. Whisk in the dissolved cornflour, cook on HIGH for 45 seconds, strain and serve in a sauce boat.

9. Garnish the pheasants with the watercress and serve with a crisp green salad.

BRAISED PHEASANT WITH CREAMED MUSHROOMS

SERVES 4

1 fl oz (25 ml) vegetable oil
2 × 1¼–1½-lb (500–750 g) pheasants, cut into 8 pieces
2 oz (50 g) butter
4 oz (100 g) carrots, sliced
4 oz (100 g) leeks, washed and sliced
2 oz (50 g) streaky bacon, rind removed and diced
1 clove garlic, peeled and diced
2 oz (50 g) celery, sliced
1½ oz (40 g) flour
1 oz (25 g) tomato purée
2 fl oz (50 ml) red wine
¾ pint (450 ml) game stock or chicken stock, hot
1 bouquet garni
1 oz (25 g) butter
8 oz (225 g) mushrooms, finely chopped
2 oz (50 g) shallots, finely chopped
1 clove garlic, crushed
Salt and freshly ground black pepper
Juice of ½ lemon
1 small glass dry sherry
4 fl oz (120 ml) double cream
Chopped parsley to garnish

1. Heat the oil in a large frying pan on a conventional stove. Add the pheasant and cook on both sides for a few moments to seal and colour the flesh slightly. Remove from the pan and place on one side.

2. Melt the butter in a large earthenware casserole dish on HIGH for 1 minute. Add the carrots, leeks, bacon, garlic and celery. Cover and cook on HIGH for 6 minutes.

3. Add the flour and tomato purée, mix in well and add the red wine and the stock.

4. Immerse the pheasant pieces in the sauce. Add the bouquet garni. Cover and cook on HIGH for 20 to 25 minutes until the pheasant is thoroughly cooked and tender.

5. Remove from the oven and leave to stand, covered, for 8 minutes.

6. Melt the 1 oz (25 g) of butter in a bowl and add the mushrooms, shallots and garlic. Season with salt and freshly ground pepper, cover and cook on HIGH for 2 minutes.

7. Add the lemon juice, sherry and cream. Mix, and cook on HIGH for 2 minutes.

8. Heap the creamed mushrooms down the centre of a warmed serving dish. Place the pheasant portions down each side of the mushroom mixture, strain the sauce over and garnish with a little chopped parsley.

JUGGED HARE

This dish requires 24 hours advance preparation. Traditionally it was created around the concept of using the blood from the hare as the main thickening agent for the sauce. Classically referred to as a 'liaison au sang'. Most good butchers and fishmongers with game licences will be able to supply you with the blood and also the liver from the hare. If, however, you find it difficult to obtain or too messy to deal with, fear not for this recipe does without it!

SERVES 4

6 oz (175 g) onions, peeled and sliced

8 oz (225 g) carrots, peeled and chopped

2 cloves garlic, peeled and chopped

2 oz (50 g) leeks, washed and sliced

4 oz (100 g) celery, washed and sliced

1 bay leaf

6 black peppercorns

1 bouquet garni

1 sprig of parsley

1¾ pints (1 l) full bodied red wine

1 × 3½-lb (1.5-kg) hare, skinned and portioned

2 oz (50 g) butter

6 oz (175 g) back bacon, rind removed and diced

1 oz (25 g) flour

1 tablespoon tomato purée

1 glass brandy

24 button mushrooms, whole

1 oz (25 g) cornflour, dissolved in cold water

4 slices white bread, cut into diamond shapes and fried

1 tablespoon chopped parsley

1. Prepare the marinade by mixing together in a very large bowl or pan the onion, carrots, garlic, leeks, celery, bay leaf, peppercorns, bouquet garni, parsley and red wine. Immerse the hare in the liquid, cover and refrigerate for at least 24 hours.

2. Remove the hare from the marinade and put to one side. Strain the liquid and discard the vegetables and herbs.

3. Place the butter in a large bowl and cook on HIGH for 1 minute. Add the bacon and cook on HIGH for a further 4 minutes.

4. Stir in the flour and tomato purée, mix well and add the brandy followed by the strained marinade. Add the hare and the mushrooms. Cover and cook for 45 minutes. Turn and reposition after 20 minutes. Check to ensure that the hare is fully cooked and then remove the hare, vegetables and bacon from the sauce and place them in a clean serving dish.

5. Whisk the dissolved cornflour into the sauce and cook on HIGH for 2 minutes. Check and adjust the seasoning if necessary.

6. Pour the sauce over the hare, vegetables and bacon and garnish with the fried bread and chopped parsley.

BRAISED PIGEON WITH CHILLED MUSCAT GRAPES

SERVES 4

2 oz (50 g) butter

6 oz (175 g) carrots, peeled and chopped

4 oz (100 g) leeks, washed and sliced

6 oz (175 g) onions, peeled and chopped

4 oz (100 g) back bacon, rind removed and diced

4 oz (100 g) celery, washed and sliced

4 pigeons, cleaned and ready for the oven

4 fl oz (120 ml) full bodied red wine

½ pint (300 ml) chicken stock, hot

1 bouquet garni

2 oz (50 g) chilled butter, cut in small cubes

8 oz (225 g) muscat grapes, chilled

1. Melt the butter in a large bowl on HIGH for 1 minute. Add the carrots, leeks, onion, bacon and celery, cover and cook on HIGH for 8 minutes.

2. Place the pigeons in the bowl. Add the wine, chicken stock and bouquet garni. Cover and cook on HIGH for 20 minutes.

3. Reposition the dish and reposition the pigeons within the sauce and cook on LOW for a further 15 minutes followed by HIGH for 15 minutes. Check to make sure the birds are cooked and tender.

4. Transfer the pigeons to a warmed serving dish and garnish with the vegetables from the sauce. Cover.

5. Remove and discard the bouquet garni, place the sauce back in the microwave and cook on HIGH for 2 minutes. Remove from the oven and whisk in the chilled pieces of butter.

6. Check and adjust the seasoning if necessary. Pour the sauce over the pigeons and garnish with four clusters of chilled grapes.

PASTA AND RICE

Pasta and rice take just as long to cook in the microwave as they do conventionally. So why microwave them? The answer is simple. It's much easier for the washer-up as they don't stick to the pan, and provided they are in a big enough bowl, the water will not boil over. And for the gourmet, each grain cooks separately.

Both pasta and rice need to be cooked in boiling water and it is far quicker to use an electric kettle for this. With pasta it is still necessary to add a little oil to the water in order to prevent the pasta sticking together. Always use a large bowl because rice and pasta will more than double in size once cooked.

When cooking pasta remember that successful microwave cookery is achieved by having similar size and shape pieces in the oven at one time, so don't mix the types. To a certain extent the success of the dish will depend on the type of pasta being cooked; the length of spaghetti and lasagne, for example, can present the cook with a logistical problem – how to fit them in the oven.

As with conventional cooking it is important to stir the pasta or rice whilst it is cooking to ensure that the pieces or grains do not stick together.

The finished result for pasta should be 'al dente' so do remember to allow a standing time for it to finish cooking.

But don't expect miracles from a microwave oven. If you need to cook large quantities, the conventional method is best. Save the microwave for smaller occasions and for re-heating pre-cooked pasta and rice.

LASAGNE

SERVES 4

8 oz (225 g) lasagne
1 tablespoon olive oil
4 oz (100 g) onion, peeled
  and finely diced
1 clove garlic, peeled and
  crushed
1 tablespoon chopped
  parsley
1 bay leaf
1 small sprig of rosemary
1 lb (450 g) ground beef
1 oz (25 g) flour
4 tomatoes, skinned,
  deseeded and finely
  chopped
1 tablespoon tomato purée
¼ pint (150 ml) beef stock,
  hot
1 glass red wine
Salt and freshly ground
  black pepper
1 oz (25 g) butter
½ oz (15 g) flour
½ pint (300 ml) milk
4 oz (100 g) Cheddar cheese,
  grated

1. Place the lasagne in plenty of boiling salted water in a large bowl, cover and cook on HIGH for 9 minutes. Leave to stand for 12 minutes and drain well.

2. Heat the oil in a large bowl. Add the onion, garlic, chopped parsley, bay leaf and rosemary. Cover and cook on HIGH for 3 minutes.

3. Add the ground beef and mix in well. Cover and cook on HIGH for 5 minutes, stirring twice.

4. Add the flour, tomatoes and tomato purée. Mix thoroughly and gradually add the hot beef stock and the red wine.

5. Season lightly with salt and freshly ground black pepper. Cover and cook on MEDIUM for 18 to 20 minutes until cooked. (Add a little more liquid if necessary – either beef stock or wine.)

6. Remove from the oven, remove the bay leaf, and leave to stand, covered.

7. Melt the butter in a small bowl. Add the flour, cook on HIGH for 1 minute, then whisk in the milk. Cover and cook on HIGH, whisking frequently, until the sauce thickens. Season with salt and freshly ground black pepper.

8. Assemble the lasagne by alternating layers of pasta and meat sauce in a shallow earthenware dish. Cover the top with the white sauce. Coat with grated cheese and brown under the grill.

LASAGNE MARINIER

8 oz (225 g) lasagne
2 oz (50 g) butter
2 oz (50 g) flour
8 fl oz (250 ml) milk, warmed
2 fl oz (50 ml) dry white wine
4 oz (100 g) prawns, cooked and peeled
6 oz (175 g) mussels, cooked
4 oz (100 g) scallops, cooked
1 tablespoon chopped parsley
Juice of ½ lemon
Salt and freshly ground black pepper
2 oz (50 g) Parmesan cheese, grated

1. Place the lasagne in plenty of boiling salted water in a large bowl, cover and cook on HIGH for 9 minutes, leave to stand for 12 minutes and drain well.

2. Melt the butter in a large bowl for 45 seconds, add the flour and mix in thoroughly to form a roux. Cover and cook on HIGH for 1 minute. Stir once during cooking.

3. Add the warmed milk, whisking continuously until smooth, cover and cook on HIGH for 2 minutes, stirring frequently. Add the wine.

4. Add the seafood, parsley and lemon juice to the sauce and season with salt and freshly ground black pepper.

5. Complete the dish by alternating layers of lasagne and sauce finishing with a top layer of sauce.

6. Cook on HIGH for 8 minutes. Top with Parmesan cheese and brown under a hot grill.

SPAGHETTI ALLE VONGOLE

SERVES 4

2 fl oz (50 ml) olive oil
2 cloves garlic, peeled and crushed
4 oz (100 g) shallots, finely diced
1 tablespoon chopped parsley
1 tablespoon chopped basil
1 bay leaf
6 whole tomatoes, skinned, deseeded and chopped

1. Heat the oil in a large bowl on HIGH for 1 minute. Add the garlic, shallots, parsley, basil and bay leaf. Cover and cook on HIGH for 4 minutes.

2. Add the tomatoes, tomato purée and wine. Cook, uncovered, on HIGH for 12 to 15 minutes to produce a sauce consistency.

3. Cook the spaghetti in plenty of boiling salted water in a pan on the stove until cooked 'al dente'. Drain into a colander. Cover and place over a pan of boiling water.

1 tablespoon tomato purée
4 fl oz (120 ml) dry white
  wine
1 lb (450 g) spaghetti
2 lb (1 kg) fresh clams,
  thoroughly scrubbed and
  discard any which are dead
Salt and freshly ground
  black pepper
Chopped parsley and basil to
  garnish

4. Add the clams to the tomato sauce. Cover and cook on HIGH for 4 to 6 minutes until the shells have opened. (It is very important to discard any shells which by this time have not opened.)

5. Add the spaghetti and using two forks mix the sauce, clams and pasta together.

6. Check and adjust the seasoning if necessary.

7. Garnish with a little chopped parsley and basil.

TAGLIATELLE NIÇOISE

SERVES 4

11 oz (300 g) tagliatelle verdi
Salt
2 oz (50 g) butter
4 oz (100 g) onions, diced
2 cloves garlic, crushed
½ teaspoon crushed black
  peppercorns
1 × 15-oz (425-g) tin
  chopped tomatoes
1 tablespoon tomato purée
2 fl oz (50 ml) dry white
  wine
1 tablespoon chopped basil
  or 1 teaspoon dried
A few drops of
  Worcestershire sauce
2 drops tabasco sauce
A pinch of sugar
Freshly ground black pepper
2 oz (50 g) anchovies, thinly
  sliced
2 oz (50 g) black olives,
  stoned
4 basil leaves

1. Place the pasta in a large bowl and add 3 pints (1.75 l) of boiling water. Season with salt, cover and cook on HIGH for 6 minutes. Cover and leave to stand.

2. Melt the butter in a large bowl on HIGH for 1 minute. Add the onion, garlic and crushed black peppercorns, cover and cook on HIGH for 3 minutes.

3. Add the chopped tomatoes, tomato purée, dry white wine and basil. Season with Worcestershire sauce, tabasco sauce, sugar, salt and freshly ground black pepper. Cover and cook on HIGH for 4 minutes.

4. Drain the pasta and add to the sauce. Gently mix together.

5. Cover and cook on HIGH for 2 minutes. Garnish with anchovies, black olives and basil leaves.

NOODLES IN LEMON, CREAM AND WALNUT SAUCE

SERVES 4

12 oz (350 g) noodles, green
  and yellow mixed
Salt
1 fl oz (25 ml) walnut oil or
  olive oil
2 cloves garlic, peeled and
  crushed
4 oz (100 g) shallots, finely
  chopped
2 oz (50 g) cooked ham,
  finely diced
1 tablespoon chopped
  parsley
3 oz (75 g) walnuts, finely
  chopped
1 teaspoon chopped sage
Juice of ½ lemon
4 fl oz (120 ml) dry white
  wine
4 fl oz (120 ml) double cream
2 fl oz (50 ml) plain yoghurt
A pinch of paprika
Freshly ground black pepper
Chopped parsley to garnish
Parmesan cheese, grated

1. Lower the noodles into plenty of boiling water in a deep casserole dish and add half the walnut or olive oil (save the rest for later) and a little salt.

2. Cover and cook on HIGH for 6 minutes until it is nearly cooked. Leave to stand, covered, for 3 minutes, by which time it should be 'al dente'. Drain and leave covered.

3. Heat the remainder of the oil in a large bowl on HIGH for 1 minute. Add the garlic and shallots. Cover and cook on HIGH for 3 minutes.

4. Add the cooked ham, parsley, walnuts and sage. Cook on HIGH for 1 minute. Pour in the lemon juice, white wine, cream and yoghurt. Season with paprika, salt and freshly ground black pepper. Cover and cook on HIGH for 1 minute.

5. Add the pasta. Gently mix together. Cover and cook on HIGH for 2 minutes until hot.

6. Garnish with the parsley and serve with grated Parmesan cheese.

SPAGHETTI BOLOGNESE

SERVES 4

1 oz (25 g) butter

2 oz (50 g) bacon, rind removed and diced

4 oz (100 g) onions, peeled and finely chopped

2 cloves garlic, peeled and crushed

2 oz (50 g) carrots, peeled and diced

2 oz (50 g) celery, washed and diced

2 oz (50 g) leeks, washed and diced

1 oz (25 g) flour

10 oz (275 g) ground beef

1 lb (450 g) ripe tomatoes, skinned, deseeded and finely chopped

3 tablespoons tomato purée

3 fl oz (85 ml) dry white wine

½ pint (300 ml) beef stock, hot

Salt and freshly ground black pepper

1 bouquet garni

1 teaspoon mixed herbs

1 quantity cooked spaghetti (page 30)

1 tablespoon grated Parmesan cheese

1. Melt the butter in a large bowl on HIGH for 45 seconds. Add the bacon, onion and garlic. Cover and cook on HIGH for 5 minutes. Stir twice during cooking.

2. Add the carrots, celery and leeks. Cover and cook on HIGH for 2 minutes. Stir in the flour and ground beef and cook, uncovered, for 2 minutes, stirring frequently.

3. Add the tomatoes, tomato purée, white wine and gradually mix in the hot beef stock. Season lightly with salt, freshly ground black pepper, bouquet garni and mixed herbs.

4. Cover and cook for 10 minutes. Stir twice during cooking.

5. Transfer the spaghetti into a warmed serving dish. Remove and discard the bouquet garni from the sauce and pour over the spaghetti. Top with Parmesan cheese and serve.

CANNELLONI WITH TOMATO AND OREGANO SAUCE

SERVES 4

1 oz (25 g) butter
4 oz (100 g) onions, peeled
  and finely diced
1 clove garlic, peeled and
  crushed
1 teaspoon oregano
6 oz (175 g) ground beef
8 oz (225 g) spinach,
  trimmed and carefully
  washed and shredded
Salt and freshly ground
  black pepper
2 oz (50 g) Ricotta cheese
2 tablespoons tomato purée

For the sauce:
1 fl oz (25 ml) olive oil
4 oz (100 g) onions, peeled
  and finely diced
1 clove garlic, peeled and
  crushed
1 teaspoon oregano
1 × 14-oz (400-g) tin
  tomatoes, chopped
2 tablespoons tomato purée
A pinch of sugar
Salt and freshly ground
  black pepper
2 drops tabasco sauce
3 drops Worcestershire
  sauce
8 cannelloni tubes

1. Melt the butter on HIGH for 45 seconds, add the onion and garlic. Cover and cook on HIGH for 3 minutes.

2. Add the oregano, ground beef and spinach, season lightly with salt and freshly ground black pepper. Cover and cook on HIGH for 2 minutes.

3. Add the Ricotta cheese and tomato purée, mix well, cover and cook on HIGH for 3 minutes. Place to one side and leave to stand, covered.

4. Prepare the sauce by heating the oil in a large bowl on HIGH for 1 minute. Add the onion, garlic and oregano, cover and cook on HIGH for 3 minutes.

5. Add the tomatoes and tomato purée. Season with a pinch of sugar, salt, freshly ground black pepper, tabasco sauce and Worcestershire sauce. Cook, uncovered, for 3 minutes, stirring occasionally.

6. Fill the cannelloni tubes with the stuffing. Lay them in a shallow casserole, pour over the sauce and cook, uncovered, for 10 to 12 minutes.

7. Allow the dish to stand, covered, for 2 minutes before serving.

PAELLA

Be sure to check not only the quality of the shellfish but also its freshness.

SERVES 4

4 oz (100 g) onions, peeled
  and finely diced
2 cloves garlic, peeled and
  crushed
1 tablespoon vegetable oil
12 oz (350 g) long grain rice
1½ pints (900 ml) chicken
  stock, hot
1 teaspoon saffron strands
Salt and freshly ground
  black pepper
4 oz (100 g) frozen peas
6 oz (175 g) cooked chicken,
  skinned and diced
6 oz (175 g) cooked mussels
4 oz (100 g) unpeeled prawns
1 red pepper, deseeded and
  finely chopped
4 oz (100 g) tomatoes,
  skinned, deseeded and
  chopped
1 tablespoon chopped
  parsley
2 oz (50 g) butter

1. Place the onions, garlic and oil in a large bowl, cover and cook on HIGH for 6 minutes.

2. Add the rice, stock and saffron and stir well. Season with salt and freshly ground black pepper. Cover and cook on HIGH for 13 minutes, stirring once half way through cooking. Remove and leave to stand, well covered, for 10 minutes.

3. Cook the peas in a bowl on HIGH for 4 minutes, add the chicken, mussels, prawns, red pepper and tomatoes. Cover and cook on HIGH for 8 minutes, stirring frequently.

4. Add to the rice and gently fork through. Add the chopped parsley and butter. Gently mix in.

5. Cover and microwave on HIGH for 3 minutes.

PILAU OF CHICKEN LIVER IN MADEIRA SAUCE

SERVES 4

1 oz (25 g) butter
1 clove garlic, peeled and
   crushed
3 oz (75 g) shallots, finely
   chopped
1 bay leaf
8 oz (225 g) basmati rice
1 pint (600 ml) chicken
   stock, hot
Salt and freshly ground
   black pepper
2 oz (50 g) butter
2 oz (50 g) shallots, finely
   chopped
1 clove garlic, peeled and
   crushed
1 teaspoon oregano
1 lb (450 g) chicken livers,
   prepared and halved
2 fl oz (50 ml) Madeira
3 fl oz (85 ml) single cream
Juice of ½ lemon
1 tablespoon chopped
   parsley

1. Melt 1 oz (25 g) of butter in a large bowl on HIGH for 45 seconds. Add 1 clove garlic, 3 oz (75 g) shallots and 1 bay leaf. Cover and cook on HIGH for 3 minutes.

2. Add the rice and chicken stock, season with salt and freshly ground black pepper. Cover and cook on HIGH for 14 minutes and leave to stand for 5 minutes, covered.

3. Melt 2 oz (50 g) of butter in a large bowl on HIGH for 45 seconds and add the shallots, garlic and oregano. Cover and cook on HIGH for 3 minutes.

4. Add the chicken livers, cover and cook on HIGH for 3 to 4 minutes. Stir gently at least twice.

5. Add the Madeira, cream and lemon juice. Season lightly with salt and freshly ground black pepper. Cover and cook on HIGH for 4 to 6 minutes until the sauce has developed.

6. Serve on a warmed dish surrounded by the pilau. Garnish with a little chopped parsley.

RISOTTO

SERVES 4

2 oz (50 g) butter

4 oz (100 g) onions, peeled
and finely diced

1 oz (25 g) red pepper,
deseeded and finely diced

1 oz (25 g) green pepper,
deseeded and finely diced

1 clove garlic, peeled and
crushed

2 oz (50 g) mushrooms,
sliced

1 teaspoon dried mixed
herbs

14 oz (400 g) long grain rice

1¼ pints (750 ml) chicken
stock, hot

4 oz (100 g) ham, diced

Salt and freshly ground
black pepper

1 tablespoon chopped
parsley

1 oz (25 g) Parmesan cheese,
grated

2 oz (50 g) butter

1. Melt the butter in a large bowl on HIGH
for 1 minute. Add the onion, red and green
peppers, garlic, mushrooms and mixed
herbs. Mix well, cover and cook on HIGH for
6 minutes.

2. Add the rice, stock and diced ham.
Season with salt and freshly ground black
pepper. Cover and cook on HIGH for 15
minutes, stirring half way through cooking.

3. Remove from the oven and leave to stand
for 6 minutes, covered.

4. Add the Parmesan cheese and butter and
gently mix in.

VEGETABLES

The trouble with vegetables is that they usually either arrive on your plate looking absolutely worn out, cooked to death, soggy and feeling very sorry for themselves or cooked 'al dente' to such a degree that they are more like a crudité.

Those days have gone! The microwave gives even the worst vegetable cook in the world the chance to present his or her guests with beautiful vegetables; and when you consider that vegetables make up nearly 60 per cent of a main meal it becomes obvious just how important it is that they are beautifully cooked.

Nearly all vegetables will cook successfully in the microwave and the distinct advantage is that they will retain their original colour (no more grey Brussels sprouts), texture and shape.

Nutritionally, microwaved vegetables come out on top. Very little water need be added as the moisture within the vegetables will produce steam, thus cooking each piece of vegetable. (This is not quite the case with older vegetables from which the moisture has dried out. In this you need to add a little more water than normal.)

Always season vegetables after cooking, as salt added before cooking dehydrates them.

As with all items to be microwaved, even-sized pieces will give the best results. So be sure to chop, cut or dice the vegetables to roughly the same size.

With flower-type vegetables, such as broccoli and cauliflower, remove or trim as much of the stalk as possible. If breaking into florets then arrange the thick stalks to the outside of the plate and heads to the centre. Apply 'tender loving cookery' to your vegetables. Turn and reposition them frequently. Those that have skins should be pricked to prevent them from bursting out all over the inside of your oven.

Cover the dish with a lid or vented microwave cling film. Remember the main cooking process when microwaving vegetables is steaming and it is essential to capture the steam as this is what tenderises them. An alternative is to cook them in roasting bags.

One of the great uses of the microwave is for re-heating pre-cooked vegetables and it does so without adversely affecting the texture or taste. The advantage of this facility becomes obvious when you consider its use for entertaining. To have the vegetables part-cooked, requiring only a few minutes to finish in the microwave, is a real life-saver.

Fresh Asparagus with Garlic and Fennel Butter

SERVES 4

1 lb (450 g) fresh asparagus
6 oz (175 g) butter
3 tablespoons chopped
    fennel leaves
1 clove garlic, peeled and
    crushed
Juice of ½ lemon
Freshly ground black pepper

1. Prepare the asparagus by trimming the ends (not the tips) and lightly remove the outer skin from the stalk. Lay them on a shallow casserole dish with the tips pointing to the centre. Add a little water, cover and cook on HIGH for 10 to 12 minutes until tender. Turn and reposition the dish after 6 minutes.

2. Drain carefully and place on a clean napkin on a serving dish.

3. Melt the butter in a small bowl on HIGH for 45 seconds. Add the fennel and garlic, cover and cook on HIGH for 2 minutes. Pour in the lemon juice and season with freshly ground black pepper.

4. Serve the sauce separately in a sauce boat.

French Beans with Garlic and Bacon

SERVES 4

10 oz (275 g) French beans,
    topped and tailed
2 oz (50 g) butter
2 oz (50 g) shallots, finely
    diced
2 cloves garlic, peeled and
    crushed
1 teaspoon chopped mint
4 oz (100 g) bacon, rind
    removed and diced
Salt and freshly ground
    black pepper

1. Place the beans in a small bowl, add a little water, cover and cook on HIGH for 12 to 14 minutes until cooked. Drain well and put to one side.

2. Heat the butter in a large shallow casserole dish on HIGH for 45 seconds, add the shallots, garlic, mint and bacon. Cover and cook on HIGH for 5 minutes, stirring frequently.

3. Add the drained beans and season lightly with salt and freshly ground black pepper. Mix well. Cover and cook on HIGH for 2 minutes until hot.

AUBERGINE EGYPTIENNE

SERVES 4

2 aubergines
1 tablespoon olive oil
1 clove garlic, peeled and
  crushed
4 oz (100 g) mushrooms,
  finely chopped
2 large tomatoes, skinned,
  deseeded and finely
  chopped
2 oz (50 g) shallots, finely
  chopped
Salt and freshly ground
  black pepper
2 oz (50 g) fresh white
  breadcrumbs
1 tablespoon freshly snipped
  chives

1. Cut the aubergine in half lengthways. Remove the inside pulp (best done with a spoon) and chop. Put the shells on to a shallow earthenware dish.

2. Heat the olive oil in a large bowl for 45 seconds. Add the garlic, mushrooms, tomatoes, shallots and chopped aubergine. Season with salt and freshly ground black pepper. Cover and cook on HIGH for 8 minutes, stirring occasionally.

3. Place the mixture neatly into the aubergine shells, cover and cook on HIGH for 6 minutes or until the aubergine is tender.

4. Sprinkle the breadcrumbs over the top of the aubergine and brown under a grill. Garnish with the snipped chives.

BABY BEETROOT IN CLARET SAUCE

SERVES 4

14 oz (400 g) baby beetroot,
  uncooked, scrubbed
1 tablespoon redcurrant jelly
¼ pint (150 ml) claret (if
  using another red wine,
  change the name of the
  sauce)
1 bouquet garni
1 heaped teaspoon arrowroot
Salt and freshly ground
  black pepper
4 mint leaves

1. Prick the beetroot and lay them on a shallow tray, cover and cook on HIGH for 7 minutes. Turn and reposition the tray during cooking. Leave to stand for 5 minutes then remove the outer skins.

2. Place the redcurrant jelly in a small bowl and cook on HIGH for 1 minute. Add the red wine and bouquet garni and cook on HIGH for 1 minute. Remove and discard the bouquet garni.

3. Dissolve the arrowroot with a little cold water and gradually whisk into the wine. Cover and cook on HIGH for 1½ minutes.

4. Season with salt and freshly ground black pepper and pour on to the beetroot.

5. Serve garnished with the mint leaves.

BROCCOLI IN CHEESE AND BACON SAUCE

SERVES 4

½ pint (300 ml) milk
1 oz (25 g) butter
2 oz (50 g) shallots, finely diced
4 oz (100 g) bacon, rind removed and diced
1 tablespoon chopped parsley
1 oz (25 g) flour
1 tablespoon chopped parsley
2 oz (50 g) Cheddar cheese, grated
1½ lb (750 g) broccoli, trimmed and cut into florets
Salt and freshly ground black pepper
1 oz (25 g) Parmesan cheese, grated

1. Heat the milk in a medium bowl on HIGH until it reaches boiling, remove and place to one side.

2. Melt the butter in a large bowl on HIGH for 1 minute. Add the shallots, bacon and chopped parsley. Cover and cook on HIGH for 4 minutes. Add the flour, mix in well and cook, uncovered, for 1 minute.

3. Gradually mix in the hot milk, whisking all the time. Cover and cook on HIGH for 2 to 3 minutes, whisking frequently. Mix in the parsley and cheese. Cover and place on one side.

4. Place the broccoli in a shallow dish, add a little water and season with salt and freshly ground black pepper. Cover and cook for 7 to 8 minutes. Turn and reposition after 3 minutes.

5. Drain off the water from the broccoli, pour the cheese and bacon sauce over the broccoli. Sprinkle with Parmesan and brown under the grill.

CAULIFLOWER POLONAISE

SERVES 4

1 large cauliflower, trimmed
and cut into florets
4 oz (100 g) butter
4 oz (100 g) fresh white
breadcrumbs
2 hard-boiled eggs, sliced and
sieved
1 tablespoon chopped
parsley

1. Rinse the cauliflower in cold running water and place in a large bowl. Add 2 tablespoons cold water. Cover and cook for 10 to 12 minutes until just cooked. Drain well and arrange neatly in a shallow serving dish.

2. Melt the butter in a shallow earthenware dish on HIGH for 1½ minutes. Add the breadcrumbs, sieved egg and chopped parsley. Mix well and cook on HIGH for 2 minutes.

3. Sprinkle the crumbs over the cauliflower and brown under a pre-heated grill.

BRAISED CELERY WITH ESSENCE OF FENNEL

SERVES 4

2 oz (50 g) butter
4 oz (100 g) bacon, rind
removed and diced
2 oz (50 g) carrots, sliced
2 oz (50 g) onion, peeled and
sliced
6 oz (175 g) fennel, washed
and diced
2 heads of celery, washed,
trimmed and cut in half
1 bouquet garni
1 pint (600 ml) chicken
stock, hot
1 tablespoon cornflour,
dissolved in a little cold
water
Salt and freshly ground
black pepper

1. Melt the butter in a large shallow earthenware dish on HIGH for 45 seconds. Add the bacon, carrot, onion and fennel. Cover and cook on HIGH for 6 minutes.

2. Arrange the celery heads neatly on top of the vegetable base. Add the bouquet garni and hot chicken stock. Cover and cook on HIGH for 12 to 16 minutes until tender. Turn and reposition the celery after 6 minutes.

3. Carefully strain off the cooking liquid into a bowl, slowly whisk in the cornflour mixture and cook on HIGH for 1 to 2 minutes until thickened. Check and adjust the seasoning if necessary. Pour the sauce over the celery and vegetables. Remove the bouquet garni and serve.

STUFFED PEPPERS

SERVES 4

1 tablespoon olive oil
3 oz (75 g) onion, peeled and
   finely diced
2 cloves garlic, peeled and
   crushed
1 lb (450 g) ground beef
Salt and freshly ground
   black pepper
2 tomatoes, skinned,
   deseeded and finely
   chopped
1 tablespoon tomato purée
2 drops Worcestershire
   sauce
1 oz (25 g) flour
½ pint (300 ml) beef stock,
   hot
4 green peppers
4 basil leaves

1. Heat the oil in a large bowl on HIGH for 1 minute. Add the onion, garlic and ground beef. Season lightly with salt and freshly ground black pepper. Cover and cook on HIGH for 6 to 7 minutes, stirring frequently.

2. Add the tomatoes, tomato purée, Worcestershire sauce and flour. Mix in thoroughly and gradually add the hot beef stock. Cover and cook on HIGH for 4 minutes then reduce to MEDIUM and cook for a further 8 minutes. Stir frequently. Check and adjust the seasoning if necessary.

3. Prepare the peppers by removing the tops with a sharp knife. Take out the seeds and core and discard. Place the hollow peppers in a shallow earthenware casserole and fill each one with the beef mixture.

4. Cover and cook on HIGH for 10 minutes until tender. Turn and reposition during cooking. Leave to stand for 3 minutes, covered, and serve each one garnished with a basil leaf.

CREAMED JACKET POTATOES

SERVES 4

**4 medium-sized potatoes,
washed and dried**
**3 oz (75 g) Cheddar cheese,
grated**
2 oz (50 g) butter
2 fl oz (50 ml) double cream
1 tablespoon snipped chives
**Salt and freshly ground
black pepper**
Freshly grated nutmeg
A pinch of paprika
4 sprigs of parsley

1. Place the potatoes on a sheet of kitchen paper, prick the skins to prevent them from bursting and cook on HIGH for 6 minutes. Turn and reposition the potatoes, replace the kitchen paper with fresh paper and cook on HIGH for a further 8 minutes. Cover the potatoes and leave to stand for 4 minutes.

2. Cut the potatoes in half lengthways and remove the flesh without damaging the shells.

3. Mash the potato and mix in the cheese, butter and cream. Season with salt, freshly ground black pepper and a little grated nutmeg.

4. Pipe the mixture back into the shells and re-heat on HIGH for 3 minutes.

5. Garnish with a light dashing of paprika and a sprig of parsley.

BOULANGÈRE POTATOES

SERVES 4

1 oz (25 g) butter
1½ lb (750 g) potatoes,
   peeled and sliced
Salt and freshly ground
   black pepper
1 large onion, peeled and
   sliced
A pinch of grated nutmeg
½ pint (300 ml) chicken
   stock, hot
2 oz (50 g) Cheddar cheese,
   grated
1 tablespoon chopped
   parsley

1. Melt the butter in a deep casserole dish. Place in a layer of potato, season lightly with salt and freshly ground black pepper, then cover with a layer of sliced onion. Repeat the process until all the onion and potato has been used. Be sure to finish with a layer of potatoes. Sprinkle the nutmeg over the top.

2. Pour on the hot chicken stock, cover and cook on HIGH for 15 to 18 minutes until the potatoes are cooked.

3. Cover with grated cheese and brown under a grill. Garnish with a little chopped parsley.

BUTTERED SPINACH WITH CREAMED NUTMEG

SERVES 4

3½ lb (1.5 kg) fresh spinach
3 oz (75 g) butter
Salt and freshly ground
   black pepper
Freshly grated nutmeg
4 fl oz (120 ml) cream

1. Remove the stalks from the spinach and discard.

2. Wash the spinach leaves in at least 4 changes of cold water. Leave to drain and then roughly chop.

3. Place the butter in a bowl large enough to hold the spinach and melt on HIGH for 1 minute then add the spinach.

4. Season lightly with salt, freshly ground black pepper and freshly grated nutmeg.

5. Cover and cook on HIGH for 5 to 6 minutes.

6. Add the cream, mix in well and cook on HIGH for 1 to 2 minutes until hot.

HARLEQUIN VEGETABLES

SERVES 4

2 tablespoons vegetable oil
4 oz (100 g) onion, peeled
   and thinly sliced
2 cloves garlic, peeled and
   crushed
4 oz (100 g) carrot, peeled
   and cut into long thin
   strips
6 oz (175 g) courgettes,
   washed, skin left on, cut in
   half lengthways and sliced
1 green pepper, deseeded and
   sliced
1 red pepper, deseeded and
   sliced
1 yellow pepper, deseeded
   and sliced
1 large aubergine, peeled and
   diced
4 tomatoes, skinned,
   deseeded and cut into thin
   slices
4 oz (100 g) baby sweetcorn
4 oz (100 g) mangetout
4 fl oz (120 ml) tomato juice
1 glass white wine (optional)
Salt and freshly ground
   black pepper
4 basil leaves

1. Heat the oil in a large casserole dish on HIGH for 1 minute. Add the onion and garlic and cook on HIGH for 3 minutes.

2. Add the carrots, courgettes, green, red and yellow peppers and aubergine. Mix well, cover and cook on HIGH for 3 minutes.

3. Add the tomatoes, sweetcorn, mangetout, tomato juice and wine if using.

4. Season with salt and freshly ground black pepper. Cover and cook on HIGH for 2 minutes.

5. Garnish with basil leaves and serve.

HUNGARIAN VEGETABLE CASSEROLE

SERVES 4

2 tablespoons vegetable oil
4 oz (100 g) onions, peeled
  and finely chopped
1 clove garlic, peeled and
  crushed
6 oz (175 g) carrots, peeled
  and diced
6 oz (175 g) swede, peeled
  and diced
1 large aubergine, peeled,
  halved lengthways, sliced
  and covered in lemon juice
6 oz (175 g) green pepper,
  deseeded and finely diced
4 tomatoes, skinned,
  deseeded and finely diced
2 tablespoons paprika
1 oz (25 g) flour
1 tablespoon tomato purée
1 glass red wine
½ pint (300 ml) vegetable
  stock, hot
1 tablespoon chopped
  parsley
4 oz (100 g) sweetcorn,
  cooked

1. Heat the oil in a large bowl on HIGH for 1 minute. Add the onions, garlic, carrots and swede. Cover and cook on HIGH for 6 to 8 minutes.

2. Add the aubergine, green pepper and tomatoes. Mix well and add the paprika and flour, tomato purée and red wine.

3. Gradually add the hot vegetable stock. Cover and cook on HIGH for 8 to 10 minutes, stirring frequently.

4. Add the chopped parsley and cooked sweetcorn and serve.

VEGETARIAN CURRY

SERVES 4

1 tablespoon walnut oil
4 oz (100 g) carrots, peeled
and finely diced
1 clove garlic, peeled and
crushed
3 oz (75 g) celery, washed
and diced
6 oz (175 g) onions, peeled
and finely chopped
2 oz (50 g) green pepper,
deseeded and diced
2 oz (50 g) red pepper,
deseeded and diced
4 tomatoes, skinned,
deseeded and finely
chopped
1 tablespoon tomato purée
Curry powder to taste
1 oz (25 g) plain flour
½ pint (300 ml) vegetable
stock, hot
1 tablespoon lemon juice
1 oz (25 g) sultanas
1 tablespoon desiccated
coconut
2 fl oz (50 ml) milk
1 banana, peeled and diced

1. Heat the oil in a large bowl, add the carrots, garlic, celery and onions. Cover and cook on HIGH for 5 minutes.

2. Add the green and red pepper and tomatoes and mix in well. Blend in the tomato purée and curry powder. Cover and cook on HIGH for 6 minutes. Mix in the flour and gradually add the hot vegetable stock, lemon juice and sultanas. Cover and cook for 5 minutes, stirring frequently.

3. Mix the desiccated coconut and milk together and leave for several minutes.

4. Add the banana to the curry and strain in the milk from the desiccated coconut.

5. Mix gently together and serve with cooked rice.

PUDDINGS AND DESSERTS

Probably the two most successful sweets that can be cooked in a microwave are the good old-fashioned steamed pudding and fruit. Either of these can be served on its own or as a base for developing a more exciting dessert. But it is possible to use the oven for quite an adventurous range of dishes providing you adhere to a few simple guidelines.

Puddings which have a high fruit or sugar content need constant attention to ensure that they don't overcook or even burn. So an eagle eye on the oven will prevent problems.

In a straight microwave (not combination) suet pastry is successful, but it must be acknowledged that with other types of pastry conventional cookery methods will produce the best results.

It is possible to get quite a nice finish with a crumble (try Rhubarb and Port crumble, page 121) providing a little brown sugar is added to the mix and once cooked it is browned under a grill. Alternatively, once cooked you can coat the top with some crushed gingernut biscuits or chopped nuts.

Chocolate requires very careful attention. Slight overtiming can have a disastrous effect on the finished result.

As mentioned before, fruit is particularly suited to microwave cookery. Take account of its shape and position it accordingly. Move and reposition it during cooking and if you are leaving the skin on then remember to prick it before cooking in order to allow the steam to escape.

DARK CHOCOLATE MOUSSE WITH WHITE CHOCOLATE SAUCE

It is hard to imagine a more sensuous combination than dark chocolate and brandy, and when that perfectly formed dark chocolate mousse sits proudly on a stunning white chocolate sauce lightly highlighted by dark chocolate feathering you'll definitely feel the earth move.

SERVES 4

1 fl oz (25 ml) water
½ oz (15 g) gelatine
3 whole eggs
2 eggs, separated
1 tablespoon sugar
1 tablespoon brandy (or
  more if you fancy)
7 oz (200 g) dark chocolate,
  broken into pieces
3 fl oz (85 ml) double cream,
  lightly whipped
6 oz (175 g) white chocolate,
  broken into pieces
2 oz (50 g) dark chocolate,
  broken into pieces
2 fl oz (50 ml) double cream

1. Place the water in a small bowl and heat on HIGH for 30 seconds. Add the gelatine and mix until dissolved and transparent.

2. Place the 3 whole eggs, 2 egg yolks and sugar in a large bowl, sit this over a bowl of hot water and whisk until the mixture becomes thick and creamy. Add the brandy.

3. Place the 7 oz (200 g) of dark chocolate in a small bowl and heat on HIGH, uncovered, for 3 to 4 minutes until it has completely melted. Stir twice during cooking. Leave to cool for a few minutes.

4. Strain the gelatine into the egg and sugar mixture, add the melted chocolate and mix gently but thoroughly.

5. Whisk the egg whites to soft peaks and use a metal spoon to fold them into the mixture. Do the same with the lightly whipped cream.

6. Transfer the mixture into individual ramekin dishes and chill for several hours.

7. Just before serving, place the white chocolate in a small bowl and the dark chocolate in another bowl and place both in the microwave. Heat on HIGH for 1 to 2 minutes until melted. (Keep a watchful eye to make sure they don't overheat.) Leave to cool for a moment and then add the cream to the white chocolate.

8. Dip the ramekins into a bowl of warm water for a few moments, making sure the water does not enter the dish, and carefully turn out the mousses on to cold plates.

9. Surround each mousse with white chocolate sauce, taking care not to splash the mousse.

10. Decorate by carefully placing a small drop of the melted dark chocolate evenly spaced around the outermost section of the sauce. Using a cocktail stick 'feather' the dark chocolate into the white chocolate sauce.

CREAM BRÛLÉE

This is a lovely upside down enriched crème caramel.

SERVES 4

12 fl oz (350 ml) double cream
A few drops of vanilla essence
4 egg yolks
1 teaspoon cornflour
4 oz (100 g) caster sugar

1. Flavour the cream lightly with the vanilla essence and cook on HIGH for 2 minutes, uncovered. Stir twice during cooking.

2. Mix the egg yolks, cornflour and 1 oz (25 g) of the sugar together in a large bowl and whisk until the mixture is thick and creamy.

3. Slowly whisk in the heated cream, a little at a time, and cook, uncovered, on HIGH for 1½ minutes. It is essential to remove the bowl every 20 seconds and give the mixture a good beating. Once finished it should be beaten for 2 minutes to ensure it is smooth, thick and creamy.

4. Transfer into 4 ramekin dishes and leave in the refrigerator to chill.

5. When required cover the top of each dish with the remaining sugar and place under a hot grill to brown.

MOCHA AND RUM CHEESECAKE

SERVES 6 TO 8

2 oz (50 g) butter
6 oz (175 g) digestive
  biscuits, crushed
1 teaspoon gelatine
3 tablespoons water
2 tablespoons instant coffee
  granules
8 fl oz (250 ml) water
1 tablespoon rum (or a little
  more if you fancy)
5 oz (150 g) soft brown sugar
1 lb (450 g) full fat soft
  cheese
½ pint (300 ml) double
  cream, lightly whipped
16 coffee beans
8 walnut halves

1. Lightly grease an 8-in (20-cm) baking tin (the best types are the loose-bottomed for this dish).

2. Melt the butter in a large bowl on HIGH for 1 minute. Add the crushed biscuits and mix together well.

3. Press the mixture into the base of the greased baking tin and chill in the refrigerator.

4. Place the gelatine in a small bowl, add 3 tablespoons of water and leave for 3 minutes. Mix well and cook on HIGH for 30 to 40 seconds until dissolved. Stir to ensure that it is lump free.

5. Add 8 fl oz (250 ml) of water to the coffee and mix in the rum and sugar. Cook on HIGH for 2 to 3 minutes and add the dissolved gelatine.

6. Leave to cool slightly and then add to the cheese. Mix well and then pass through a food processor, blender or fine sieve.

7. Using a metal spoon fold in half of the lightly whipped cream and once well mixed in pour on top of the biscuit base.

8. Place in the refrigerator for 4 hours to allow the cheesecake to set.

9. To finish, remove the cheesecake from the tin and decorate with piped cream, coffee beans and walnut halves.

SPOTTED DICK WITH WHISKY AND HONEY CREAM

I resisted including my favourite sweet, Bread and Butter Pudding, in this book in favour of my second favourite. That wonderful quote 'to eat well in England one should eat breakfast three times a day' should have 'and spotted dick twice' added to it.

I like to serve small portions with a little whisky and honey cream, (and follow it with a two-hour nap).

SERVES 4

3 oz (75 g) self-raising flour
A pinch of salt
3 oz (75 g) fresh brown
  breadcrumbs
3 oz (75 g) shredded suet
2 oz (50 g) soft light brown
  sugar
6 oz (175 g) currants
3½ fl oz (100 ml) milk
½ pint (300 ml) double
  cream
1 glass whisky, to taste
2 tablespoons runny honey

1. Mix the flour, salt, breadcrumbs, suet, sugar and currants in a large bowl. Add the milk gradually, stopping once the mixture has reached dropping consistency.

2. Transfer into a 1½-pint (900-ml) pudding basin and cover loosely with microwave cling film. Cook on HIGH for 5 minutes. Remove and leave to stand for 5 minutes.

3. Put the cream, whisky (you must resist drinking it) and honey into a bowl and whisk lightly. Once it has gained body, stop whisking.

4. Turn the pudding out on to a warm serving dish and transfer the cream into a pretty bowl.

STEAMED GOLDEN SYRUP PUDDING

No matter how hard I try it is impossible to resist including this 'made for the microwave' sweet. I think it should be a compulsory dish served at every dinner party!

SERVES 4

6 tablespoons golden syrup
2 oz (50 g) butter or
margarine, softened
4 oz (100 g) soft brown sugar
2 eggs, lightly beaten
4 oz (100 g) self-raising flour,
sifted
2-3 tablespoons milk

1. Pour the syrup into a 2-pint (1.2-l) pudding basin and tilt it so that the syrup covers the sides as well as the bottom. (A 30-second blast on HIGH will soften the syrup and help speed the process.)

2. Place the butter in a mixing bowl and beat in the sugar, a little at a time, until the mixture becomes light and fluffy.

3. Gradually beat in the eggs until well blended. Use a metal spoon to fold in the flour. Add the milk, 1 tablespoon at a time and mix well. The batter should be soft and smooth and should drop easily from a spoon.

4. Transfer the batter into the pudding dish and smooth the top surface.

5. Cook on HIGH, uncovered, for 6 minutes or until the pudding has risen and is quite firm.

6. Leave to stand for 2 minutes, covered, and check to ensure it is cooked by inserting a knife or trussing needle down the centre. The blade should be clean and free from batter when removed. If not, cook on HIGH for a further 1 minute.

7. Turn the pudding out on to a warmed plate.

VANILLA SPONGE PUDDING WITH MINT AND RASPBERRY SAUCE

SERVES 4

2 oz (50 g) plain flour, sifted
2 oz (50 g) caster sugar
¾ teaspoon baking powder
A pinch of salt
A few drops of vanilla
  essence, to taste
1 oz (25 g) margarine
1 egg
1½ fl oz (40 ml) milk
12 oz (350 g) raspberries,
  sieved
2 oz (50 g) caster sugar
2 teaspoons cornflour
1 tablespoon cold water
½ teaspoon lemon juice
4 mint leaves, washed and
  finely chopped

1. Mix the flour, sugar, baking powder, salt, vanilla essence, margarine, egg and milk together until smooth.

2. Put the batter into individual pudding moulds and cook on HIGH for 3½ to 5 minutes until firm to touch. Turn and reposition the moulds twice during cooking. Remove and leave to stand, covered, for 2 minutes.

3. Place the raspberries and sugar in a bowl. Mix together the cornflour and water and add to the raspberries with the lemon juice. Mix in well.

4. Cook on HIGH for 2½ minutes, stirring frequently.

5. Add the chopped mint leaves and mix in well.

6. Turn the puddings out on to a warm serving dish and serve with the sauce.

APPLE AND BRAMBLE DELIGHT

SERVES 4

1 large dessert apple, peeled,
   cored and sliced
8 oz (225 g) brambles, picked
   and washed
2 tablespoons water
1 oz (25 g) lemon rind, grated
1 oz (25 g) orange rind,
   grated
½ pint (300 ml) custard
   sauce, cooled
4 fl oz (120 ml) double
   cream, lightly whipped

1. Place the apple, brambles and water in a large bowl, cover and cook on HIGH for 7 minutes until the fruit is cooked.

2. Pass through a food processor, blender or a fine sieve. Add to the custard and add the lemon and orange rind.

3. Fold in the cream, either completely or partly thus giving a streaky appearance to the sweet.

4. Transfer into serving dishes and chill before serving.

PEACH UPSIDE DOWN PUDDING

SERVES 4

5 oz (150 g) butter
1 oz (25 g) soft brown sugar
4 peach halves
4 glacé cherries, halved
4 oz (100 g) caster sugar
2 eggs, lightly beaten
4 oz (100 g) self-raising flour,
   sifted

1. Place 1 oz (25 g) of butter and the brown sugar in a lightly greased 2-pint (1.2-l) soufflé dish. Cook on HIGH for 45 seconds.

2. Lay the peach halves neatly on the bottom of the dish and fill any spaces with the cherries.

3. Mix the remaining butter with the caster sugar in a large bowl and beat until light and fluffy.

4. Gradually beat in the eggs and use a metal spoon to fold in the flour. Transfer the mixture to the soufflé dish, completely covering the peach halves.

5. Cook, uncovered, on HIGH for 7 to 8 minutes. Turn the dish round after 3 minutes.

6. Leave the pudding to stand for 4 minutes before turning out.

7. Serve with cream or hot creamy custard.

POACHED PEARS WITH HOT CHOCOLATE AND GRAND MARNIER CREAM

Stand well clear – this is unadulterated seduction cuisine!

SERVES 4

4 ripe dessert pears, peeled and stalks left on
8 oz (225 g) plain chocolate
2 fl oz (50 ml) Grand Marnier
Finely grated zest of 1 orange
3 fl oz (85 ml) single cream or plain yoghurt

1. Place the pears upright on a deep plate and cook, uncovered on HIGH for 5 minutes or until tender. Remove and leave to cool.

2. Place the chocolate in a small basin and cook on HIGH for 3 to 4 minutes until it has completely melted. Stir after 2 minutes.

3. Add the Grand Marnier, orange zest and cream or yoghurt. Mix well together and pour over the pears.

LEMON AND KUMQUAT PUDDING

SERVES 4

2 oz (50 g) soft margarine
2 oz (50 g) caster sugar
1 egg, beaten
4 oz (100 g) self-raising flour
Juice and finely grated rind of 1 lemon
3 oz (75 g) kumquats, finely chopped
1-2 tablespoons milk

1. Beat the margarine, sugar, egg and flour until smooth.

2. Add the lemon zest, juice and chopped kumquats. Mix in thoroughly.

3. The batter should be of a consistency capable of dropping off a spoon. Use sufficient milk to correct the consistency.

4. Transfer to a lightly greased 1-pint (600-ml) pudding basin and smooth the surface. Cook on HIGH, uncovered, for 5 to 7 minutes until the top feels firm.

5. Leave to stand, covered, for 6 minutes and then turn out on to a warmed serving plate.

6. Serve with cream, custard or ice-cream.

CHILLED LEMON AND PISTACHIO SOUFFLÉ

SERVES 4

2 tablespoons water
1 tablespoon gelatine
5 oz (150 g) caster sugar
7 fl oz (200 ml) hot water
3 eggs, separated and the
  whites whisked to a peak
Zest of 1½ lemons, cut into
  very fine strips
Juice of 1½ lemons
½ pint (300 ml) double
  cream, lightly whipped
2 oz (50 g) pistachio nuts,
  peeled and chopped

1. Lightly grease a 1-pint (600-ml) soufflé dish and surround the outside of the dish with greaseproof paper so that it rises to 2 in (5 cm) above the height of the dish. Secure with string or an elastic band and then very lightly grease the inside of the paper above the top of the dish.

2. Pour the water into a small bowl and add the gelatine. Leave to stand for a few minutes, mix in gently with a fork and then cook on HIGH for 20 to 25 seconds (just enough time to enable it to dissolve).

3. Add the sugar, water and egg yolks and mix in thoroughly. Cover and cook on LOW for 5 to 7 minutes. This stage requires tender loving care – the mixture must not boil and requires very regular stirring.

4. Reserve a little lemon zest for decoration. Add the remainder to the mixture with the lemon juice and stir thoroughly. Set aside to cool and thicken.

5. Before it shows signs of setting, add the whisked egg white using a metal spoon.

6. Reserve a little cream for decoration, and fold in the remainder. Add half the chopped pistachio nuts.

7. Pour the mixture into the prepared soufflé dish and chill for at least 2 hours before serving.

8. Carefully remove the greaseproof paper and decorate the top of the soufflé with a little piped cream, a sprinkling of lemon zest and the remaining chopped pistachio nuts.

BAKED CINNAMON APPLES

SERVES 4

3 oz (75 g) seedless raisins
3 oz (75 g) sultanas
2 oz (50 g) angelica, washed
1 teaspoon cinnamon
2 fl oz (50 ml) brandy
2 oz (50 g) demerara sugar
4 medium-sized cooking
   apples
1 oz (25 g) butter
4 tablespoons water

1. Mix together the fruit, angelica, cinnamon, brandy and sugar.

2. Remove the cores from the apples and make a hole of appropriate size to take the filling.

3. Make an incision around the apple skin about two-thirds of the way up.

4. Place the apples in an ovenproof dish, fill the holes with the fruit mixture and put a little butter on top of each.

5. Pour the water into the base of the dish, cover loosely and cook on HIGH for 6 to 8 minutes. Turn and reposition the dish half way through.

6. Leave to stand for 8 minutes, covered. This dish 'demands' custard.

RASPBERRY FOOL

SERVES 4

4 level teaspoons cornflour
½ pint (300 ml) milk
1½ lb (750 g) raspberries,
   washed
3 level tablespoons caster
   sugar
1 small glass kirsch
½ pint (300 ml) double
   cream, lightly whipped
4 raspberries
4 mint leaves

1. Mix a little milk with the cornflour to form a smooth paste. Add the remainder of the milk and whisk. Cook on HIGH for 4 to 5 minutes or until the sauce has thickened, stirring frequently. Leave to stand, well covered, until cold.

2. Pour the raspberries into a food processor, blender or through a fine sieve and add to the cold sauce. Sweeten with the sugar to taste, add the kirsch and mix well.

3. Using a metal spoon fold the whipped cream into the raspberry mixture. Transfer into individual dishes and chill until required.

4. Decorate with the raspberries and mint leaves.

CASSEROLE OF BANANAS WITH EXOTIC FRUITS

For this dish you will need 2 ramekins per person. The idea is that in one you have a salpicon (diced) exotic fruit selection and in the other a hot casserole of bananas. To eat you simply put a spoonful of fruit into the casserole and enjoy the taste sensation.

SERVES 4

3 passion fruit, scooped
2 kiwi fruit, peeled and diced
1 mango, peeled and diced
6 kumquats, chopped
  (or any unusual
  combination that takes
  your fancy)
1 glass kirsch
½ pint (300 ml) milk
2 eggs
1 level tablespoon
  granulated sugar
2 drops vanilla essence
2 bananas

1. Prepare the fruit salad, cutting the fruit into fairly small pieces. (Remember it's going to be placed into a small ramekin so large pieces or chunks would not look right.) Place in the ramekins and top each one with a little kirsch.

2. Heat the milk in a large bowl on HIGH for 2 minutes or until hot.

3. Lightly whisk the eggs, sugar and vanilla essence together and then strain back into the bowl.

4. Cook on HIGH for 1 minute and then LOW for 5 minutes or until the sauce begins to show body. (You can test this by dipping a spoon in. When removed the sauce should coat the back of the spoon.) It is important to whisk several times during cooking.

5. Remove and leave to stand, well covered.

6. Peel the bananas and cut lengthways. Then cut into smaller pieces across and place in a small bowl. Cook on HIGH for 30 seconds and transfer into the sauce.

7. Place the casserole of bananas into individual ramekins. To serve, sit a ramekin of banana and one of fruit with a serviette on a main course plate and place a flower head in between the two dishes – sensuous cuisine or what?

RHUBARB AND PORT CRUMBLE

SERVES 4

1½ lb (750 g) rhubarb,
   washed and trimmed
2 fl oz (50 ml) port
1 tablespoon redcurrant jelly
4 oz (100 g) soft brown sugar
4 oz (100 g) butter, cold and
   cubed
6 oz (175 g) flour, sifted

1. Slice the rhubarb into 1½-in (4-cm) pieces and place into a deep baking dish. Add the port, redcurrant jelly and 1 oz (25 g) of the sugar. Cover and cook on HIGH for 3 to 4 minutes until the rhubarb becomes tender to touch. Stir frequently during cooking.

2. Rub the butter into the flour, with tender loving care, until the mixture has a fine sandy texture. Gently mix in the remaining sugar.

3. Sprinkle the crumble mixture on to the cooked fruit and press it gently but firmly into place.

4. Cook on HIGH for 10 to 12 minutes until it feels firm to touch. Turn the dish several times during cooking.

5. Leave to stand for 6 minutes, covered, and then place under a pre-heated grill to brown.

6. Serve with cream, honey yoghurt or piping hot custard.

ORANGES IN BITTER COINTREAU SYRUP

This simple-to-prepare sweet is an elegant addition to a selection for a dinner party and won't have you whizzing around for hours before your guests arrive.

SERVES 4

8 small oranges
2 lemons
6 oz (175 g) granulated sugar
¼ pint (150 ml) water
1 small glass fresh orange
 juice
1 small glass cointreau
4 mint leaves

1. Remove the zest from the oranges and cut it into very thin strips. Cut away the white pith from the oranges and place them in a round shallow dish.

2. Remove the zest from the lemons and cut it into very thin strips. Cut away the white pith from the lemons, take out the lemon segments and arrange them in between the oranges. Put to one side.

3. Place the sugar, water, orange and lemon zest and orange juice in a bowl and cook, uncovered, on HIGH for 8 minutes. Keep checking the syrup and stir frequently.

4. Add the cointreau and mix well. Pour over the fruit. Garnish with mint leaves. Serve hot or chilled.

BAKED GOODS

Most cooks would prefer to adhere to the traditional methods of baking in order to achieve good results and I confess to being one of them. When baking conventionally the goods are placed in a pre-heated oven, the food cooks by heat being transferred from the cooking container to the inside of the goods and from the outer surfaces of the food. At the same time dry heat caramelises the outer layers turning them brown – therein lies the big difference.

However, it is possible to produce a most acceptable product providing you follow a few guidelines and remember that the distinct advantage of baking in a microwave oven (not a combination type) is speed.

Where possible bake in round dishes, as oblongs and squares have edges which, if not protected, can lead to those areas overcooking.

Do not use flour to line a baking tin as you might with the conventional method as the finished product will result in a nasty floury substance which will adhere to the outside of the cake once cooked.

Select ingredients which will look good once 'microbaked'. Chocolate cake is a good example. For those 'baked' goods which look pale and insipid, top them with chopped nuts or a dusting of icing sugar.

Foods taken from the microwave will continue to cook for a little while so bear this in mind when testing to see if a cake is done. The denser in texture the longer the cooking process will continue once removed from the oven.

But for me the general rule is – if it doesn't look good cooked in the microwave, bake it!

CHERRY AND ALMOND BISCUITS

This recipe will produce delightfully 'tender' biscuits which will soon disappear in any household.

MAKES 24 BISCUITS

4 oz (100 g) butter
4 oz (100 g) caster sugar
1 large egg, lightly beaten
6 oz (175 g) plain flour, sifted
2 oz (50 g) ground almonds, sifted
4 oz (100 g) glacé cherries, chopped

1. Lightly grease a large microwave baking tray.

2. Place the butter and sugar in a bowl and beat until light and fluffy.

3. Gradually add the egg and beat well into the creamed mixture. Then fold in the flour, ground almonds and glacé cherries.

4. Spoon 8 biscuit-sized portions on to the baking tray. Leave enough space between each one for them to spread out. Cook on HIGH for 1½ to 2½ minutes or until the biscuits are dry on the surface and firm to touch.

5. Remove from the oven and transfer on to a wire rack to cool.

6. Repeat the process using the remaining mixture.

MUESLI SLICES

Delicious muesli snacks that you can merrily chew to your gums' delight.

MAKES 10 SLICES

4 oz (100 g) butter
6 oz (175 g) runny honey
2 oz (50 g) dried peaches, chopped
2 oz (50 g) dates, chopped
3 oz (75 g) sunflower seeds
4 oz (100 g) rolled oats
½ teaspoon salt
4 oz (100 g) brown sugar
1 egg
1 oz (25 g) self-raising flour, sifted

1. Place the butter and honey in a large bowl and cook on HIGH for 2½ minutes.

2. Add all the ingredients, except the egg and flour. Mix thoroughly.

3. Beat the egg into the mixture and add the flour, mixing thoroughly.

4. Transfer on to a lightly greased microwave baking tray and cook on HIGH for 8 to 10 minutes.

5. Leave to stand for 6 minutes and then use a palette knife to mark the muesli into slices. Leave to cool then cut into slices.

FLAPJACKS

MAKES 24

6 oz (175 g) butter
1½ oz (40 g) caster sugar
2 oz (50 g) soft brown sugar
6 tablespoons golden syrup
A pinch of salt
10 oz (275 g) rolled oats
3 oz (75 g) grape nuts

1. Lightly grease a large shallow dish.

2. Place the butter, caster sugar and soft brown sugar in a large bowl. Cook on HIGH for 1½ minutes.

3. Add the golden syrup, salt, oats and grape nuts. Mix in well until blended.

4. Place the mixture in the prepared dish and smooth over the surface.

5. Cook on HIGH for 5 to 6 minutes, turning the dish after each minute. Leave to cool.

6. Cut into small triangles or squares or whatever takes your fancy.

DARK CHOCOLATE FUDGE FINGERS

It is well worth investing in good quality chocolate for these little goodies. The better the raw ingredients the nicer the finished product.

MAKES ABOUT 14 FINGERS

4 oz (100 g) dark chocolate
4 oz (100 g) butter
1 lb (450 g) icing sugar
2–3 tablespoons milk (the
 children's version)
or 2–3 tablespoons brandy
 (the adult's version)

1. Place all the ingredients in a bowl and cook on HIGH for 2 to 3 minutes until the chocolate has melted. Beat until smooth.

2. Pour into a 7 × 7-in (18 × 18-cm) tin. Mark the surface with a palette knife to form the portions and leave to cool in the refrigerator.

3. Cut into portions and serve.

WALNUT AND CHERRY CAKE

MAKES A 2 LB (1 KG) CAKE

6 oz (175 g) butter
6 oz (175 g) soft brown sugar
3 eggs, lightly beaten
8 oz (225 g) plain flour and
 1½ teaspoons baking
 powder sifted together
½ teaspoon salt
2–4 tablespoons milk
3 oz (75 g) walnuts, chopped
2 oz (50 g) glacé cherries,
 chopped
1 oz (25 g) icing sugar

1. Line a 2-lb (1-kg) loaf dish with greaseproof paper and lightly grease the paper.

2. Cream the butter and sugar until it becomes light and fluffy and add the eggs a little at a time. Beat in vigorously.

3. Using a metal spoon fold in the sifted flour, baking powder and salt.

4. Add the milk, a little at a time, until the mixture is at dropping consistency and mix in the chopped walnuts and cherries.

5. Transfer into the prepared loaf dish and smooth the surface with a knife.

6. Protect the ends of the cake from overcooking by shielding the edges of the dish with narrow strips of foil. Place on an upturned plate and cook on HIGH for 7 minutes.

7. Leave to stand for 6 minutes before turning out on to a wire rack to cool.

8. Dust a little icing sugar over the top of the cake before serving.

TRADITIONAL GINGERBREAD

MAKES A 10 × 6 IN
(25 × 15 CM) CAKE

2 oz (50 g) butter
2 oz (50 g) treacle
½ oz (15 g) caster sugar
4 oz (100 g) plain flour, sifted
½ teaspoon ground ginger
½ teaspoon mixed spice
½ teaspoon bicarbonate of soda
1 small egg, beaten

1. Lightly grease a 2½-pint (1.5-l) deep oblong dish.

2. Put the butter into a large bowl and cook on HIGH for 45 seconds. Add the treacle and caster sugar and cook on HIGH for 1 minute. Leave to cool slightly.

3. Add the flour, ginger, mixed spice and bicarbonate of soda and mix thoroughly. Blend the egg into the mixture and give it a harsh beating.

4. Transfer the mixture into the prepared dish and place on an upturned plate. Cook on HIGH for 3½ to 4 minutes. Turn and reposition the dish after each minute.

5. Leave to stand for 5 minutes and then remove from the dish on to a wire rack and leave to cool before serving.

FRUIT CAKE

This is a fairly rich recipe and just like all good fruit cakes it is best made well in advance and stored for later use. It will certainly benefit from 6 weeks storage in an air-tight container. Mind you, if yours is like our house it will be lucky to last a week without someone's sticky fingers getting to it!

MAKES A 6 IN (15 CM)
CAKE

6 oz (175 g) butter
6 oz (175 g) soft brown sugar
Grated rind of 1 lemon
3 eggs, lightly beaten
7 oz (200 g) plain flour, sifted
¼ teaspoon ground mixed spice
¼ teaspoon ground cinnamon
1 lb (450 g) mixed dried fruit
3 oz (75 g) glacé cherries
1 oz (25 g) walnuts, chopped
1 oz (25 g) flaked almonds
1 tablespoon black treacle
2 fl oz (50 ml) brandy or rum

1. Lightly grease and line a 6-in (15-cm) deep round cake tin.

2. Cream the butter and sugar until light and fluffy. Add the lemon rind, mix well and beat in the eggs a little at a time.

3. Use a metal spoon to fold in the flour, mixed spice and cinnamon.

4. Add the remaining ingredients and mix gently.

5. Transfer into the prepared cake tin and gently tap to ensure that it is even.

6. Cook on LOW for 35 to 40 minutes. Turn and reposition the cake every 6 minutes.

7. Test to see if it is cooked by carefully inserting a thin skewer into the centre of the cake. If it is cooked the skewer will come out clean and free from batter.

8. Leave to cool slightly and then remove from the tin on to a wire rack.

9. Store until matured. (It does the cake no harm to pour on a little brandy or rum every now and then.)

ORANGE AND CARROT CAKE

MAKES A 7 IN (18 CM)
CAKE

4 oz (100 g) butter
4 oz (100 g) dark brown
  sugar
2 medium eggs, beaten
Juice of 1 orange
Grated zest of 1 orange
¼ teaspoon ground cloves
¼ teaspoon grated nutmeg
¼ teaspoon cinnamon
4 oz (100 g) carrots, peeled
  and grated
4½ oz (120 g) self-raising
  flour
1 oz (25 g) ground almonds
1 oz (25 g) caster sugar

For the topping:
4 oz (100 g) cream cheese
2 oz (50 g) icing sugar
2 tablespoons lemon juice

1. Lightly grease a 7-in (18-cm) ring mould.

2. Cream the butter and brown sugar together until they are fluffy. Add the eggs, a little at a time, beating vigorously.

3. Add the orange juice, zest, spices and grated carrots. Mix well.

4. Use a metal spoon to fold in the flour and almonds until well blended.

5. Transfer into the prepared mould and smooth the surface. Sprinkle the caster sugar on top.

6. Cover with microwave cling film and cook on HIGH for 8 to 10 minutes. Turn the cake every 2 minutes.

7. Remove the microwave cling film and leave the cake to stand for 10 minutes. Turn out on to a wire rack to cool.

8. Beat the topping ingredients together and use to ice the cake when cool.

CHOCOLATE SPONGE

This cake should be eaten the same day as it will lose its freshness quickly.

MAKES A 7 IN (18 CM)
CAKE

6 oz (175 g) caster sugar
6 oz (175 g) soft margarine
1½ oz (40 g) cocoa powder
**5 oz (150 g) self-raising flour,
  sifted**
1 teaspoon baking powder
3 tablespoons milk
3 eggs

1. Lightly grease a 7-in (18-cm) round, 3½-in (9-cm) deep tin.

2. Mix together all the ingredients in a large bowl and beat until smooth.

3. Transfer the mixture into the prepared cake tin. Place on an upturned plate and cook on HIGH for 3 minutes. Reposition the cake and cook for a further 3 minutes, then reposition again and cook for a final 3 minutes.

4. Leave to stand for 4 minutes and then turn it out on to a wire rack and leave to cool.

5. Decorate the top with chocolate fudge icing or sifted icing sugar.

SAVOY TEA CAKES

MAKES 8

2 oz (50 g) butter
4 fl oz (120 ml) milk
½ teaspoon dried yeast
¼ teaspoon sugar
12 oz (350 g) granary flour
1 teaspoon salt
1 egg, lightly beaten
2 oz (50 g) currants
1 oz (25 g) chopped mixed
   peel
4 oz (100 g) cracked wheat

1. Put the butter into a bowl and cook on HIGH for 1 minute. Add the milk and stir.

2. Add the dried yeast and sugar, cover and leave in a warm place for 12 to 15 minutes until the mixture begins to 'bubble'.

3. Put the flour and salt into a large bowl, make a well in the centre and add the yeast mixture, the beaten egg, currants and mixed peel. Mix to form a dough.

4. Turn the dough out on to a lightly floured surface and knead until it becomes smooth and springy. Put back into the bowl, cover with a clean damp tea towel and leave in a warm place (back to the airing cupboard!) until it has doubled in size, 1 to 1½ hours.

5. Remove from the bowl on to the floured surface and knead again to remove all the air bubbles.

6. Cut into 8 equal pieces and form each one into a flat oval. Place these on a lightly greased dish and cover with the damp tea towel. Put back into the warm place until they double in size.

7. Dampen the surface of the tea cakes and sprinkle them with the cracked wheat.

8. Cook for about 5 to 6 minutes and test to see if they are cooked. They should sound hollow when tapped. Leave to stand for 6 minutes and transfer to a wire rack to cool completely.

WHOLEMEAL LOAF

MAKES 4 1 LB (450 G)
LOAVES

1½ pints (900 ml) water, at
  room temperature
1 teaspoon malt
2 tablespoons dried yeast
3 lb (1.5 kg) plain wholemeal
  flour
2 tablespoons brown sugar
4 teaspoons salt
4 tablespoons cracked wheat

1. Lightly but thoroughly grease 4 × 1-lb (450-g) microwave loaf tins.

2. Pour ½ pint (300 ml) of water into a bowl, add the malt and sprinkle in the dried yeast. Mix with a fork and leave in a warm place for 10 to 12 minutes.

3. Place the flour, sugar and salt in a large bowl and mix thoroughly. Make a well in the centre and pour in the water and yeast mixture and the remaining 1 pint (600 ml) of water. Mix to form a firm dough.

4. Turn the dough out on to a lightly floured surface and knead it firmly until it becomes smooth and springy.

5. Place the dough back in the bowl. Cover with a clean damp cloth and leave it in a warm place (in the airing cupboard with the clean knickers and socks is as good as anywhere) until it doubles in size. This can take from 30 minutes up to 1 hour depending on the temperature.

6. Turn the dough out on to the floured surface and knead it very firmly. Be as aggressive as you like and make sure that you remove all the air bubbles. Once it becomes smooth and springy then it's ready.

7. Divide the dough into 4 equal-sized pieces and drop into the prepared loaf tins. Press down lightly and cover with a damp cloth. Place back in the warm place until each loaf has doubled in size.

8. Lightly wet the tops of the loaves and sprinkle on the cracked wheat.

9. Cook each loaf separately for 5 to 6 minutes.

10. Remove from the tins and place each one upside down on a piece of absorbent paper and cook on HIGH for 1 to 2 minutes. They should sound hollow when tapped, once cooked.

SODA BREAD

MAKES A 7 IN (18 CM) ROUND LOAF

10 oz (275 g) wholemeal flour
6 oz (175 g) plain flour, sifted
1 level teaspoon salt
1 level teaspoon bicarbonate of soda
½ oz (15 g) butter
10 fl oz (300 ml) milk
2 level teaspoons cream of tartar
1 level teaspoon soft brown sugar

1. Lightly grease a large flat dish.

2. Mix together the flours, salt and bicarbonate of soda and gently rub in the butter. Make a well in the centre.

3. Place the milk in a separate bowl, add the cream of tartar and sugar and mix well until dissolved.

4. Pour this into the well in the flour and mix to form a dough. (It may be necessary to add more liquid; if so use milk.)

5. Knead the dough on a lightly floured board until it becomes smooth and then roll it out to form a 7-in (18-cm) round and transfer it to the prepared dish.

6. Mark a cross on the top and sprinkle with a little wholemeal flour.

7. Cook on HIGH for 10 to 11 minutes. Turn and reposition at least every 2 minutes during cooking. Check to ensure that it is cooked, transfer to a wire rack and leave to stand for 5 minutes.

QUICK CUISINE

Perhaps one of the greatest assets of this 'high tech culinary whizzbox' is its ability to produce, in a few minutes, an exciting supper snack. The urge to jump up and conjure a tasty little number during a boring part of a film you are watching at home is well within your grasp.

This whole area is one for you to play with and develop your own ideas and recipes. Simply take a main ingredient which requires very little cooking and add to it other quick-cook items which you feel will blend well with the main source of the dish, but more importantly that you and your family and guests will enjoy.

BUTTER FRIED MUSHROOMS WITH CHIVE AND YOGHURT DRESSING

SERVES 4

2 oz (50 g) butter
2 oz (50 g) snipped chives
1 clove garlic, peeled and
   crushed
2 oz (50 g) bacon, rind
   removed and diced
8 oz (225 g) button
   mushrooms, quartered
Juice and rind of ½ lemon
4 fl oz (120 ml) plain yoghurt
Salt and freshly ground
   black pepper
Snipped chives to garnish

1. Melt the butter in a large bowl on HIGH for 1 minute. Add the chives, garlic and bacon. Cover and cook on HIGH for 3 minutes.

2. Add the mushrooms, cover and cook on HIGH for 3 minutes. Pour in the lemon juice, lemon rind and yoghurt. Mix thoroughly and season with salt and freshly ground black pepper.

3. Cook, uncovered, for 1 minute and serve garnished well with freshly snipped chives.

MUSHROOMS ITALIAN STYLE

SERVES 4

2 oz (50 g) butter
2 oz (50 g) shallots, finely
   chopped
1 clove garlic, peeled and
   crushed
8 oz (225 g) mushrooms,
   sliced
2 oz (50 g) Italian salami,
   diced
1 teaspoon oregano
1 teaspoon chopped parsley
2 fl oz (50 ml) dry white
   wine
¼ pint (150 ml) cream
Salt and freshly ground
   black pepper
2 tablespoons Parmesan
   cheese, grated

1. Melt the butter in a large bowl on HIGH for 1 minute. Add the shallots and garlic. Cook on HIGH for 1 minute.

2. Add the mushrooms and salami, cover and cook on HIGH for 2 minutes. Stir after 1 minute.

3. Add the oregano, parsley, wine and cream and season lightly with salt and freshly ground black pepper. Mix well. Cover and cook on HIGH for 2 to 3 minutes until the sauce has thickened.

4. Top with Parmesan cheese and brown under a grill.

POTTED SHRIMPS

This simple recipe makes a lovely informal snack or elegant dinner party starter, simply modify the garnish to suit the occasion.

SERVES 4

8 oz (225 g) butter, cut into cubes
1 sprig of rosemary
8 oz (225 g) shrimps, cooked and peeled
Cayenne pepper to taste
1 tablespoon chopped parsley

1. Place half the butter in a large bowl and add the rosemary. Cover and cook on HIGH for 1 to 2 minutes until the butter melts.

2. Add the shrimps, cayenne pepper and parsley. Cover and cook on LOW for 2 minutes. Remove the rosemary and transfer the shrimps into four individual ramekin dishes. Put to one side.

3. Melt the remaining butter in a large bowl on HIGH for 2 minutes until melted. Place to one side to allow the solids to settle at the base of the bowl then carefully spoon the clear yellow butter (clarified) over the potted shrimps.

4. Once they begin to set place them in the refrigerator and chill. Garnish according to taste.

TOMATO PRAWNS WITH WARM GARLIC BREAD

SERVES 4

2 oz (50 g) butter
2 oz (50 g) onion, finely chopped
1 clove garlic, peeled and crushed
1 tablespoon freshly chopped basil or ½ teaspoon dried
½ teaspoon crushed black peppercorns

1. Melt the butter in a large bowl on HIGH for 1 minute. Add the onion, garlic, basil and crushed peppercorns. Cover and cook on HIGH for 3 minutes.

2. Add the prawns, bay leaf and chopped tomatoes. Cover and cook on HIGH for 2 minutes.

8 oz (225 g) prawns, cooked
   and peeled
1 bay leaf
4 large tomatoes, skinned,
   deseeded and finely
   chopped
1 tablespoon tomato purée
1 fl oz (25 ml) dry white
   wine
A pinch of sugar
Salt and freshly ground
   black pepper
Loads of warm garlic bread

3. Add the tomato purée and wine and season with sugar, salt and freshly ground black pepper. Cover and cook on HIGH for 1 to 2 minutes.

4. Remove the bay leaf and serve with lashings of warm garlic bread.

WARM QUEEN SCALLOP AND BACON SALAD WITH WALNUT DRESSING

Queen scallops are wonderful! Such tender young flesh with a unique flavour. In the Isle of Man (where the finest can be tasted) they are simply called Queenies. So sweet!

SERVES 4

4 radicchio leaves
4 frisée leaves
4 batavia leaves
1 head chicory, sectioned
   into leaves
3 tablespoons walnut oil
1 tablespoon sherry vinegar
2 oz (50 g) butter
12 queen scallops, shelled
4 oz (100 g) bacon, grilled
   and chopped
1 tablespoon chopped
   chervil
Juice of ½ lemon
Salt and freshly ground
   black pepper
1 oz (25 g) walnuts, chopped
4 pieces chervil

1. Wash, dry and tear the salad leaves in small neat pieces.

2. Mix the walnut oil and sherry vinegar together to form the dressing and dip the leaves in, gently shake off the surplus and arrange the leaves decoratively on serving plates.

3. Melt the butter in a shallow dish on HIGH for 1 minute. Add the scallops, cover and cook on HIGH for 1 minute. Turn them over after 30 seconds and add the chopped grilled bacon, chopped chervil and lemon juice.

4. Season with salt and freshly ground black pepper and place on the salad leaves. Scatter the chopped walnuts over and around at random. Highlight the dish with the chervil leaves and serve.

SCRAMBLED EGG WITH PIQUANT KIDNEYS

This is a superb combination but is at its best when timed perfectly. Scrambled eggs is one of those dishes that demands to be cooked and eaten as close together as possible. The rule, in general, for cooking scrambled egg in the microwave is to 'cook with the heart and not with the watch'. So put the Gucci away for this dish and keep an eagle eye on the glass door of your oven.

SERVES 2

1 teaspoon oil
1 oz (25 g) onion, peeled and chopped
2 oz (50 g) lambs' kidneys, skinned, core removed and chopped
½ teaspoon Dijon mustard
2 drops Worcestershire sauce
1 fl oz (25 ml) red wine
A pinch of cayenne pepper
Salt and freshly ground black pepper
4 eggs
3 tablespoons double cream
1 oz (25 g) butter
Chopped parsley

1. Heat the oil in a large bowl on HIGH for 45 seconds. Add the onion and kidney. Cover and cook on HIGH for 3 minutes.

2. Add the mustard, Worcestershire sauce, red wine and cayenne pepper. Cover and cook on HIGH for 3 to 4 minutes.

3. Season with salt and freshly ground black pepper. Cover well and place on one side to stand.

4. Whisk the eggs, cream and butter in a large bowl and season with salt and freshly ground black pepper. Cook uncovered on HIGH for 2 minutes. Whisk thoroughly and cook on HIGH for a further 1 minute and then whisk again. Cook on HIGH for a final minute and then whisk before serving. (Cook with the heart, remember.)

5. Place the scrambled egg on a plate and spoon a well in the centre into which place the piquant kidneys. Garnish with a little chopped parsley.

Tomato Forestière

SERVES 4

4 large firm tomatoes
2 oz (50 g) butter
1 clove garlic, peeled and
  crushed
3 oz (75 g) mushrooms,
  finely chopped
2 oz (50 g) fresh
  breadcrumbs
1 oz (25 g) Parmesan cheese,
  grated
2 tablespoons chopped
  parsley
Juice of ½ lemon
2 tablespoons dry white
  wine
Salt and freshly ground
  black pepper

1. Slice the tops from the tomatoes, take out the insides and discard.

2. Melt the butter on HIGH for 1 minute. Add the garlic, cover and cook on HIGH for 2 minutes. Add the mushrooms and cook on HIGH for 2 minutes.

3. Stir in the breadcrumbs, cheese and parsley. Add the lemon juice and wine. Season lightly with salt and freshly ground black pepper.

4. Spoon into the tomato cases and cook on HIGH for 2 minutes. Turn and reposition them after 1 minute.

5. Leave to stand for 1 minute before serving.

Hot Cinnamon Grapefruit

SERVES 4

2 grapefruit
2 fl oz (50 ml) sherry
4 oz (100 g) brown sugar
1 tablespoon cinnamon

1. Cut the grapefruit in half and loosen the segments with a knife. Place each grapefruit half in a serving dish.

2. Mix the sherry, sugar and cinnamon together in a bowl, cover and cook on HIGH for 2 minutes.

3. Spoon the sherry mixture over the grapefruit and place them in the oven. Cook on HIGH for 3 minutes. Turn and reposition the dishes after 1½ minutes.

AVOCADO WITH CRAB AND CUCUMBER TOPPING

SERVES 4

2 avocados, ripe
Juice of ½ lemon
4 oz (100 g) crab meat, white and brown mixed
A pinch of paprika
2 oz (50 g) cucumber, peeled and finely diced
2 fl oz (50 ml) double cream
Salt and freshly ground black pepper
1 teaspoon dill or fennel, chopped
4 wedges of lemon

1. Cut the avocado pears in half and remove all traces of the stone. Using a teaspoon, scoop out the flesh. Then with a sharp knife cut it into small even-sized pieces. Cover with lemon juice to prevent the flesh from discolouring.

2. Add the crab meat, paprika and cucumber. Mix in the cream and season with salt and freshly ground black pepper.

3. Spoon back into the empty avocado shells, place on a plate with the narrowest part of the avocado to the centre. Cover loosely with microwave cling film and cook on HIGH for 4 minutes.

4. Serve in warm individual dishes garnished with dill or fennel and lemon wedges.

SOMERSET MULE

So called because of its kick! Drink with caution!

MAKES 1½ PINTS (900 ML)

1 pint (600 ml) oakvat cider
4 fl oz (120 ml) dry white wine
4 fl oz (120 ml) fresh orange juice
1 measure calvados
1 measure vodka
1 oz (25 g) caster sugar
A pinch of nutmeg
12 apple slices

1. Place all the ingredients except the apple slices into a large jug. Heat on HIGH for 4 minutes, stirring twice during this time.

2. Serve garnished with the apple slices.

HOT SPICED CHOCOLATE

MAKES 1½ PINTS (900 ML)

**2 oz (50 g) plain chocolate
(good quality)**
1 pint (600 ml) milk
2 tablespoons rum
½ teaspoon cinnamon
**1 oz (25 g) plain chocolate,
grated**

1. Break the chocolate into small pieces and place in a jug. Cook on HIGH for 2 to 3 minutes, stirring twice.

2. Add the milk, mix well and cook for 4 to 5 minutes, stirring twice.

3. Pour in the rum and mix well. Serve in mugs with the cinnamon and grated chocolate sprinkled over the surface.

MULLED WINE

Christmas lights, carols, mince pies and a glass of mulled wine. All's right with the world!

MAKES 1½ PINTS (900 ML)

6 fl oz (175 ml) water
¾ pint (450 ml) red wine
**¼ pint (150 ml) fresh orange
juice**
2 oz (50 g) caster sugar
6 tablespoons brandy
½ teaspoon cinnamon
10 orange slices
4 mint leaves

1. Place all the ingredients except the orange slices and mint leaves in a large bowl. Stir well and heat on HIGH for 5 minutes.

2. Garnish with the orange slices and mint leaves floating in the wine.

INDEX